FIT

CAT

521 646 52 8

FIT
CAT

TIPS & TRICKS to Give Your Pet a LONGER, HEALTHIER, HAPPIER Life

Arden Moore

APPLE

First published in the UK in 2015 by
Apple Press
74-77 White Lion Street
London N1 9PH

www.apple-press.com

ISBN: 978 1 84543 578 3

Conceived, designed and produced by
Quid Publishing
Level 4, Sheridan House
114 Western Road
Hove BN3 1DD
England

Design by Clare Barber

Printed in China

10 9 8 7 6 5 4 3 2 1

I dedicate this book to my cat-adoring
friends, Jocelyn Shannon and
Audrey Pavia; my niece, Alicia Hayes;
and the fine felines past and present in
my life: Corky, Samantha, Little Guy,
Callie, Murphy, Zeki and Casey.

Contents

Foreword

As a veterinary surgeon, I meet lots of pet owners. I meet them on a daily basis, every type of pet owner you can imagine. As a writer, blogger and the president of the Cat Writers' Association, I meet a fair number of writers and broadcasters as well. However, I meet very few people that are dedicated to their pets and willing to share their vast knowledge of pets and pet care in the same way as Arden Moore.

I've had the pleasure of being acquainted with Arden for a while. I have the distinct pleasure of being able to call her a friend. She is a quite talented writer, something I do not claim lightly. In Arden's case though, I can state that with complete honesty.

I've found Arden to be loyal and straightforward in all her dealings. I've featured her writing on my own blog, something that I take very seriously. I do not welcome guest posts or feature content by just any writer. The writer needs to have not only the qualifications to be able to claim expertise in the field on which they are writing but also writing skills that allow the conveyance of the message in clear, concise, easy to understand terms. Arden qualifies on all counts.

In the pages to follow, you'll benefit from Arden's extensive knowledge and experience. Your investment in this book is something you'll never regret. I urge you to take full advantage.

Thank you for your attention. Enjoy the book! I know you're in for a treat.

Sincerely,

LORIE HUSTON

LORIE HUSTON, DVM

Lorie is a Certified Veterinary Journalist, President of the Cat Writers' Association, and a finalist in the 2014 Pet Industry Woman of the Year Awards.

Introduction

Think of this book as your customised guide to all things C–A–T! With step-by-step guidelines, tips and tricks as well as insights about your cat, this book is designed to ensure your feline friend enjoys a long, healthy life.

Merely a generation ago, most cats lived outdoors. They dined on food scraps or commercial food filled with grains. Many worked as mousers, ridding barns and homes of unwanted rodents. Too many only saw a vet maybe once after being adopted for a first round of vaccinations. You've come a long way, kitty! Felines today enjoy the benefits of a pet revolution. Careers have been created out of this fascination with felines and other pets. In more recent times, people established themselves as professional pet groomers, certified cat behaviourists, pet first aid instructors and vets who only specialise in caring for cats.

Admit it, our felines influence us in what we buy, where we live and how we decorate our homes. Paw through the pages of this book to discover more about decorating options such as 'catios' (outdoor enclosures specifically built for indoor cats) and feline 'superhighways' for living rooms. Discover, too, how to stretch your family budget without sacrificing the quality of care for your cat. Find out clever tips to outfox your feline so you can enjoy a sound night's sleep and how to maintain harmony between your cat and any other family pet.

You can also learn how to teach your cat impressive performance tricks and experience good-quality playtime to improve the relationship with your feline.

I am honoured to be your guide for you and your 21st-century cat. Ever since I was a toddler, I've shared my life with a cat or two. My feline friendship began with a cool Siamese named Corky, who joined me swimming in our garden lake and never turned down a blue gill I reeled out of the lake. My current cats answer to the names Murphy and Zeki. At 15, Murphy is an ageless feline wonder who still exhibits kitten-like energy and purrs like a diesel truck. At 5, Zeki wows audiences as my confident feline assistant whenever I give cat behaviour presentations or hands-on pet first-aid classes. She is a certified therapy cat and accomplished travel kitty by car and aeroplane.

Our cats truly are the cat's whiskers! They delight us. They fascinate us. They love us. It is now time to cuddle up with your cat and read through these pages.

Arden Moore

CHAPTER 1
General Health

How Healthy Is Your Cat?

Tap into your senses of sight, touch and smell to keep tabs on your tabby and identify what is normal for her in order to catch early warning signs of any possible health concerns.

An annual veterinary examination is a must for every cat, but it is only the starting point in looking after your cat's health. Once a week, pick a quiet time away from distractions and devote 5 to 10 minutes to inspect your cat from nose to tail. These weekly at-home health checks can highlight potential problems early. Special training is not required, just observational skills and a commitment to your cat's general wellbeing.

Your duty is to recognise what is normal and healthy for your cat, and to pay attention to any changes. Don't forget that changes in your cat's routine – from how much she eats or drinks, her elimination schedule, when and how long she sleeps, and her energy level – can be indications that she isn't feeling her fit feline self. Be wary that cats are masters at masking their pain and need your help in identifying subtle changes from their normal routines.

There are 10 at-home health checks for your cat's face and body that are fast, easy and effective. Jot down the vital signs and record any changes so that you can report them to your vet.

1 **CHECK YOUR CAT'S EYES.**
Healthy eyes are bright, with no signs of any red or yellow tinge to the white of the eye (also known as the sclera) or the lining of the eye. The pupils should be symmetrical and should quickly constrict to a bright light and grow larger in a dark room. There should not be any discharge (mucus) oozing from the tear ducts.

2 **CHECK YOUR CAT'S EARS.**
Your cat is blessed with keen hearing. Her erect ears can pivot independently and zero in on sounds from varying distances and volume levels. Inspect the outer and inner ear for any signs of redness, scrapes, excessive wax or smell. A cat suffering with ear mites, for example, will have what looks like coffee grounds inside the ear.

3 **CHECK YOUR CAT'S NOSE.**
A healthy feline nose may be black, pink or spotted, depending on the breed. Any nasal discharge should be clear and not excessive amounts. Contrary to what you may have heard, a healthy nose can be wet or dry. But it should never be extremely dry and cracked or extremely moist with thick mucus.

4 **CHECK YOUR CAT'S GUMS AND TEETH.**
Most cats sport pink gums, a sure sign of health. Gently open your cat's mouth and assess your cat's gum condition. Take your finger and gently press against the gum above your cat's canine tooth. This is called the capillary refill test (CRT). Press and release. If circulation is healthy, the colour should return to pink within 2 seconds. Next, inspect your cat's 30 teeth for any signs of missing or cracked teeth and finally, take a whiff. You should not be able to detect a rancid odour from your cat's breath. Foul-smelling breath could be a sign of periodontal disease or an ailing organ, such as the liver or kidneys.

5 CHECK YOUR CAT'S RESPIRATORY RATE.

Count the number of breaths your cat takes per minute. Make sure she is at rest when you do this. Each respiration equals one inhalation and one exhalation (look for the chest to rise and fall). A panting cat – one who is cooling down from zooming inside your home, for example – will breathe more rapidly than normal. When your cat is at rest, her breathing should be even and regular, not laboured, and approximately 20 to 30 breaths per minute (see box).

6 CHECK YOUR CAT'S HEART RATE.

With your cat standing, press your open palm against the rib cage over the heart and count how many heartbeats you feel per minute (their pulse). Or press your two middle fingers gently on the inner side of your cat's hind leg, towards the groin, to feel for the femoral artery. Count the beats for 1 minute. A normal heart beats from 140 to 220 per minute at rest (see box).

7 CHECK YOUR CAT'S HYDRATION.

Gently lift some of your cat's skin from the back of her neck and release. The skin should spring back immediately. If it does, this means that your cat's skin has good elasticity and serves as a sign that she is getting enough fluids and is not dehydrated.

8 CHECK YOUR CAT'S COAT AND BELLY.

Glide your open palm down your cat's body from the base of the tail to the head and then gently in the other direction to lift the coat hair. Do you see any small dark brown or black spots in your cat's body? These may be fleas, and they can make your cat miserable. Matted hair can also be painful and lead to skin irritations. Examine for any bumps around the spine and palpate the abdomen to feel for any lumps or skin tags or signs of discomfort.

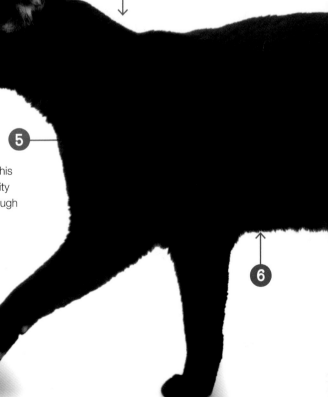

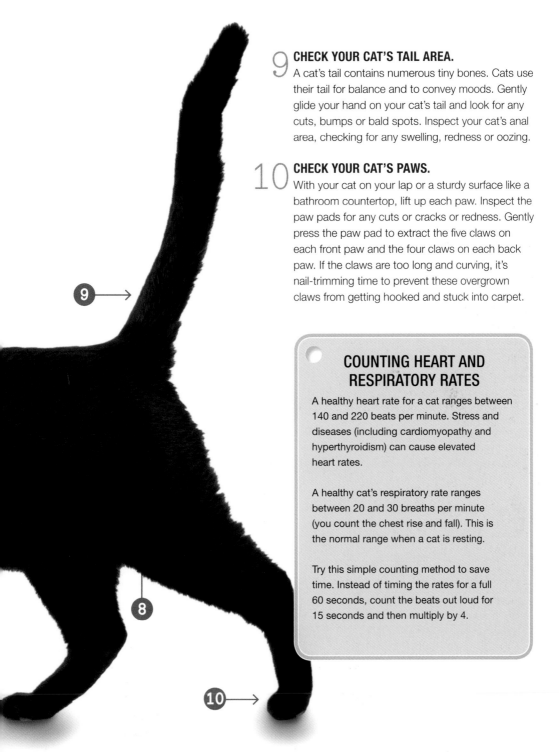

9   CHECK YOUR CAT'S TAIL AREA.

A cat's tail contains numerous tiny bones. Cats use their tail for balance and to convey moods. Gently glide your hand on your cat's tail and look for any cuts, bumps or bald spots. Inspect your cat's anal area, checking for any swelling, redness or oozing.

10   CHECK YOUR CAT'S PAWS.

With your cat on your lap or a sturdy surface like a bathroom countertop, lift up each paw. Inspect the paw pads for any cuts or cracks or redness. Gently press the paw pad to extract the five claws on each front paw and the four claws on each back paw. If the claws are too long and curving, it's nail-trimming time to prevent these overgrown claws from getting hooked and stuck into carpet.

COUNTING HEART AND RESPIRATORY RATES

A healthy heart rate for a cat ranges between 140 and 220 beats per minute. Stress and diseases (including cardiomyopathy and hyperthyroidism) can cause elevated heart rates.

A healthy cat's respiratory rate ranges between 20 and 30 breaths per minute (you count the chest rise and fall). This is the normal range when a cat is resting.

Try this simple counting method to save time. Instead of timing the rates for a full 60 seconds, count the beats out loud for 15 seconds and then multiply by 4.

Visiting the Vet

Book your feline in for a thorough health examination at the vet at least once a year. Twice a year is even better to ensure any conditions are picked up early when treatment can be most effective and costs less.

Since cats sport a long-standing reputation for not showing any outward signs of pain or discomfort, whenever possible you need to take on a new role of pet detective. Your mission is to gather as many clues as possible to determine if a visit to the veterinary clinic is warranted – or if you should monitor your cat at home for a day or so.

Emergency Situations

These dire health emergencies demand contacting your vet immediately and rushing your cat to the clinic:

* Your cat is unconscious and you cannot hear her pulse or heartbeat.
* Your cat has severe difficulties breathing.
* Your cat's gums are white or bluish (healthy gums should be bubble-gum pink).
* Your cat broke her leg misjudging the distance or height of a jump.
* Your cat is spurting bright red blood, possibly indicating a severed artery.
* Your cat is hit by a vehicle.
* Your cat is bitten by a snake or poisonous spider (such as the false widow spider), or stung on the face by bees or wasps and exhibits laboured breathing.
* Your cat fell from a balcony or open window two storeys or higher.
* Your cat suffered slashing by claws and bite wounds in a fight with another cat.
* Your cat's eye is protruding out of its socket or appears enlarged. Or you notice one eye is fully dilated and the other is not, suggesting a neurological condition.
* Your male cat is straining to urinate and crying, indicating a blockage.
* Your cat strikes her head hard or has a seizure.

CHECKING YOUR CAT'S TEMPERATURE

To record your cat's temperature, gently insert a digital pet thermometer (lubricated with petroleum jelly) into the rectum. Another option is to use an ear thermometer that works by measuring infrared heat waves emitting from the eardrum area. Place the thermometer deep into the horizontal ear canal to obtain an accurate reading.

A healthy temperature ranges between 37.9°C to 39.17°C (100°F to 102.5°F).

Take your cat to your vet's surgery if her body temperature is below 37.2°C and above 40°C (less than 99°F or above 104°F).

Your cat has suffered second- or third-degree burns on her body.

Your cat has a fever with an elevated temperature above 40°C (104°F).

Your cat staggers, walks in circles, and tilts his head to one side, indicating a neurological condition.

Your cat has detectable blood in a runny or soft stool.

Situations to Monitor

Some signs of ill health in your feline are not classed as dire, but they still merit a call to your vet who will decide if you should bring in your cat immediately or observe your cat and bring her in the next day to be examined:

Your cat begins coughing or sneezing constantly.

Your cat has experienced diarrhoea or vomiting for more than 24 hours and is lethargic.

Your cat suddenly starts drinking water excessively.

Your cat's eyes are cloudy or she starts to squint.

Your cat has a rash and is persistently scratching or chewing at her body.

Your cat sports an unusual lump that is red, painful to the touch, and warm.

Your cat has a bloody nose.

Your cat declines two meals in a day.

Your cat starts drooling.

Your cat has been limping for a day, but is still bearing weight on the leg.

Other General Health Issues

Finally, here are some less obvious indications that your cat may not be feeling completely well. These require observation for a couple days, then for you to report your findings to your vet:

Your normal fastidious cat is now occasionally urinating or defecating outside the litter box – possible early signs of FLUTD (feline lower urinary tract disorder).

You notice that your cat's urinary clumps in the litter box are enlarging and she is demanding that you refill the water bowl more often – possible indicators of diabetes.

Your cat has suddenly lost a lot of weight in a month.

Your cat is becoming very vocal, even howling loudly.

Your usually frisky cat is sleeping more and displaying disinterest in playing favourite games, like stalking and pouncing on a feather wand toy.

Your cat's once-clear eyes are now weepy with excessive discharge from the eyes and even from the nose.

Your cat is no longer regularly grooming herself and her coat has become dry or matted.

Your once-mellow cat is suddenly full of energy, begging for food and losing weight – possible early signs of hyperthyroidism (an overactive thyroid).

Work With Your Vet

Unlike your family physician, veterinary surgeons face a special challenge: their patients can't talk to them or tell them where they hurt or how they feel. That's why providing specific information to your vet during the visit is so crucial. Your details can help narrow down the possible reasons behind why your cat is ailing and also potentially prevent huge veterinary bills. Follow this handy checklist to help you get the most out of your next visit to the vet – for your cat's sake.

By working in harmony with your vet, your cat stands a better chance of being diagnosed early and treated more effectively.

BEFORE YOUR VISIT TO THE CLINIC
BRING OUT THE CARRIER.

The night before, bring out your cat's carrier, open the door and pop in a tasty treat for her to find and enjoy. Some cats flee the scene when they see you bring out the carrier because they equate it with riding in a car and heading to the clinic. This strategy will make the carrier less threatening.

LIMIT ESCAPE ROUTES.

The morning of your visit, casually start closing off rooms in your house, like the bedroom and closets. This prevents your cat from positioning herself under your bed just out of your reach. Or, feed your cat that morning in a bathroom with the door closed (and be sure to place her litter box and water bowl there, too). When it is time to head to the veterinary clinic, you can easily fetch your cat.

To get your cat feeling safe and comfortable travelling inside her carrier, feed one meal inside it once a week. Leave the carrier's door open.

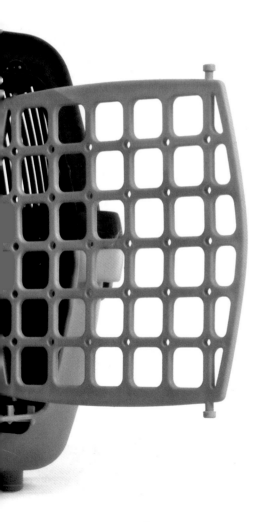

COMPILE A LIST OF QUESTIONS.

Don't try to rely on your memory while you are in the consulting room. Instead, bring a list of questions you want your vet to address about the care of your cat. Ask about your cat's diet, toileting habits, hair coat quality and any other issues of concern. Finally, check in advance whether your vet needs you to bring a fresh stool sample sealed in a plastic bag.

NOTE DOWN FEEDING HABITS.

Bring a list of the specific brand of food your cat eats, the exact amount you feed her daily, as well as any treats. If you can bring the bag that contains the list of ingredients, that's even better. Don't forget to include a note of all medications, herbs and vitamin supplements that your cat may take.

CHART ANY HEALTH ISSUE.

Write down in advance all the 'clues' you've detected about the change in your cat's behaviour. For example, record the date when she started vomiting, having diarrhea or started to skip using the litter box. Name the time when your cat's appetite started to wane or accelerate.

GET THE APPOINTMENT TIME RIGHT.

Strive to pick the first appointment of the day, if possible, or the first appointment after lunch to avoid waiting delays in the lobby.

ALLOW FOR TRAVEL TIME.

Allow time for unexpected traffic delays to ensure you arrive at the clinic on time. Show up at least 10 minutes early to fill out any necessary paperwork. Make sure your cat is secure inside a carrier before exiting your home and entering the car to prevent escapes. Be sure the carrier is secured to your vehicle's seatbelt in the middle seats for her protection. Also, pack a bath towel (see page 22).

If your cat is a bit skittish or easily frightened, consider taking her to a cat-only veterinary clinic so she doesn't have to contend with dogs in the lobby.

AT THE CLINIC
TURN OFF YOUR MOBILE PHONE.
Practise phone-off etiquette in the consulting room so that you can focus fully on your cat's examination.

USE A TOWEL FROM HOME.
Place the bath towel you have packed on the stainless steel examination table to make it more comfortable for your cat to be examined.

SPEAK UP.
Be your cat's health advocate by discussing your concerns with your veterinary surgeon. Write down the answers. However, when your vet is performing a physical examination, especially when listening to your cat's heart and lungs, resist engaging in small talk so your vet can get a good reading on your cat's vital signs.

ASK FOR HELP.
If your cat needs to be given medication at home, her recovery depends on you complying by giving her medicine (pills, liquid or injections) as prescribed. Ask the vet staff to show you the best medicine-giving technique.

SEEK TREATMENT OPTIONS.
Discuss cost and possible side effects of any medication before deciding on the best care option for your cat. Also inquire about any free medication samples that may be available to save you on your veterinary bill.

PLAY IT SAFE.
Make sure your cat is safely secured inside the carrier before exiting the consulting room so that she doesn't escape in the lobby or out the clinic's door.

BOOKING A MOBILE SERVICE

Cats need and deserve being checked over at least once a year by a vet. But that doesn't mean that they have to be put in carriers, shuttled in vehicles and examined at a veterinary clinic. It is worth seeking out agencies which offer all the services of a traditional vet but from the comfort of your home. These mobile services are fairly new. Consider making an appointment if the following apply:

➤))))● You have a cat who gets so stressed outside the comforts of your home that she urinates, defecates and/or vomits inside her carrier during transport. Why put her through this unnecessary stress?

➤))))● Your cat behaves sweetly at home but transforms into an angry cat who hisses, swats and attempts to bite inside a veterinary consulting room. Such behaviour prevents a vet from doing a thorough examination.

➤))))● You have several pets and want to avoid the logistical nightmare of booking multiple appointments to provide them routine care.

➤))))● You have a feline who is in fragile health. She may be terminally ill or very old.

➤))))● You don't drive.

➤))))● You are in ill health.

➤))))● You desire more personal care for your pet. A mobile vet can see first-hand how your home environment may contribute to your cat's health condition.

➤))))● Many procedures performed at a veterinary clinic can be performed in your home by a mobile vet. Physical examinations, blood and urine collection for lab work, vaccinations, microchipping for identification purposes, administering subcutaneous fluids, trimming nails and cleaning ears are among the services that can be done by a vet in your home. However, surgical procedures and taking X-rays must be undertaken at the clinic.

Medicine Time

Veterinary scientists are developing more effective medicines in pill, liquid and other forms. Your job is to learn how to administer any prescribed medication to your cat, calmly and effectively.

You sigh with relief after your vet examines your ailing cat and tells you that she will make a complete recovery. But then your vet brings out a bottle of pills or liquid medicine and begins instructing you on how to give your cat the right dose each day. Perhaps you begin to panic, as you envision an unwanted struggle between you and your cat at medicine-giving time. It doesn't have to be that way. Before reaching for the medicine bottle, put yourself in a patient but purposeful frame of mind. This is important because your cat can read – and respond to – your emotional state.

Giving medicine to your cat can be stress free, for the both of you. Where you dish out the medicine is crucial. Select a location that thwarts feline escapes, such as a bathroom where you can close the door. Position your cat so that her rear end is against a wall to prevent her from backing up and escaping. You can also wrap your cat in a bath towel (see page 130).

Before you give the medicine, have the tools you need already in the bathroom. These include a syringe with water or tuna juice, tinned tuna or your cat's favourite treat and possibly, a pill gun. At the end of a session make sure to give a small treat as a reward, open the bathroom door and allow your cat to exit on her own.

Pill-Giving Guide

1 Place the pill in the pill gun and add a tiny amount of canned cat food (or other food that your cat likes) on the tip of the pill gun to hide the pill.

2 Sit behind your cat or position her against a wall so that she cannot back up. Place your fourth and fifth fingers behind your cat's skull to keep her from moving her head.

3 Tilt your cat's head back and open her mouth. Insert the pill gun into your cat's mouth and deposit the pill at the back of the tongue.

4 Remove the pill gun and quickly close your cat's mouth while continuing to tilt her head up. Massage her throat gently to induce swallowing. Scratch behind her ears (if she likes that) to make it a positive experience.

5 Follow up by carefully squirting a syringe filled with water or tuna juice into the side of your cat's mouth to ensure the pill has been properly swallowed and does not get stuck in her oesophagus. Take care to leave your cat's head level when giving this liquid.

Liquid Medicine Guide

1 Develop a positive association by placing your cat's favourite treats, such as tinned tuna, on the syringe tip for her to lick off.

2 Then load the syringe with tuna juice for your cat to swallow as a trial the first time round. Open your cat's mouth, insert the syringe from the side and squirt in the liquid (remember to hold her head to get her to accept being slightly restrained). Because liquids are more likely than pills to enter the trachea, keep your cat's head level.

3 Follow up immediately with the medicine-filled syringe at its proper dose. You can also squirt the liquid medicine onto the roof of the mouth if your cat accepts having her mouth wide open.

4 Remove the syringe and close her mouth so that she can't spit out the medicine.

MEDICINE-GIVING OPTIONS

Consult your veterinary surgeon about seeing if the three-times-a-day dose can be converted to one-time a day, or if you can split the pill for easier swallowing, use a pill gun or pulverise it without compromising the effectiveness of the medicine.

The bottom line is that your cat needs medicine and needs you to comply with your vet's instructions. Your feline friend is counting on you to return to a healthy state.

Make medicine-giving time a relaxed, rewarding experience for your cat so she starts to associate getting medicine with getting tasty treats.

CHAPTER 2

Knowing Your Cat

Basic Characteristics

To understand your cat's innate characteristics and really appreciate how he thinks requires some general knowledge of cat ancestry.

Recent scientific studies reveal that lions, tigers and other wild cats share 95 per cent of DNA with house cats, all members of the Felidae family. There is a direct DNA link between the mighty lion in the jungle and the tame tabby purring peacefully in your lap! In fact, big cats in the wild and domesticated felines share these rather similar characteristics:

- All cats are obligate carnivores. They rely primarily on meat to fuel their bodies.
- All cats embrace this feline mantra: hunt, catch, kill, eat, groom, sleep. The only difference is the type of prey. Lions hunt deer and other wildlife, while house cats stalk feather wand toys.
- All cats possess powerful, fast-acting muscles necessary to chase down prey.
- All cats, interestingly, lack genetic receptors to detect sweetness.
- All cats sport tongues covered with horny papillae (spiky barbs that aid in grooming).
- All cats (except the cheetah) have the capability to retract their sharp claws at rest and protract their claws for hunting and for fighting.
- All cats have five toes on each front foot and four toes on each hind foot, with the exception of polydactyl cats (a genetic mutation that causes more toes on each foot).
- All cats have keen night vision that enables them to spot moving objects in dim light.

Understanding the origins of your cat's behaviour can only be a good thing. Your purring house cat shares far more in common with the mighty jungle lion than you realise.

🐾 Hunt, catch, kill, eat, groom, sleep is a sequenced mindset shared by domesticated cats and those in the wild.

🐾 All cats use their cone-shaped ears like radar to zoom in on a wide range of sounds, especially high-frequency sounds made by mice, rats and other rodents.

🐾 All cats prefer to survey their surroundings from elevated perches. For the African leopard, that often means hanging on a high tree branch. For your tabby, that may mean the top of your refrigerator.

🐾 All cats rub and scratch on objects to mark their territory with scent. The subordinate wild lion in a pride will body rub a higher-ranked lion for food. Your tabby will rub against your legs when you are in the kitchen in hopes of scoring dinner early.

Feline Moods

Cats are candid about what they want and when they want it. They don't lie or deceive. And, they certainly don't apologise like some dogs might. Cats ooze with cat-itude so deciphering core emotions is important.

In order to properly read your cat's emotions, you need to consider the entire package. The specific environment or situation also helps to put any of these feline clues into context. Here is a closer look at eight primary feline emotions directed towards people.

AFFECTION
WHAT TO LOOK FOR:

Cats in loving moods will lower their heads and lightly tap your forehead (known as a 'head bump', 'butt' or 'bunt'). Some deliver soft-eyed winks to you by half-closing both eyes at once. Another way a cat displays admiration for a favourite person is by twitching the top third of his hoisted tail as he approaches. Overall, the cat's body is relaxed and you may hear steady purring. The cat may also jump in your lap or sit very close next to you.

To identify cat-to-cat friendship, look for bodies to touch as the two cats pass one another in a hallway or look for them to briefly intertwine tails. Cat pals also engage in mutual grooming sessions. Some also happily share a cat bed, squeezing in together.

HOW TO RESPOND:

Try giving your cat a few soft winks back and lowering your head so he can more easily do the 'head butt'. Speak his name in a friendly, upbeat tone and treat him to some hand scratching under his chin.

AGGRESSION
WHAT TO LOOK FOR:

Aggressive runs the gamut; from being fear-related, territorial, protective of resources, to pain-related such as suffering from a medical condition or injury. A cat full of ire or in pain gives warning signals before biting or clawing. Look for a tensing of the muscles, thumping of the tail, flattening of the ears, skin twitching and vocalising unhappily in a distressed tone.

HOW TO RESPOND:

Stop petting your cat if he is on your lap and he starts to show any of the above signs. Stand up and walk away. If your cat bites your hand, the best way to release his bite grip is to relax your hand and move it towards his mouth. Do not attempt to yank your hand quickly away because he is apt to tighten the grip and bite deeper (as he is genetically wired to do when he captures a mouse or other prey).

Never physically hit an aggressive cat because such action may escalate this behaviour and seriously impact your relationship, making him mistrust you. Redirect these cats with toys such as feather wands that encourage erratic movements towards which they can re-channel their energies.

Just like us, cats feels joy, fear, pain and contentment. To read your feline's mood, study their body language, postures, vocalisations and actions.

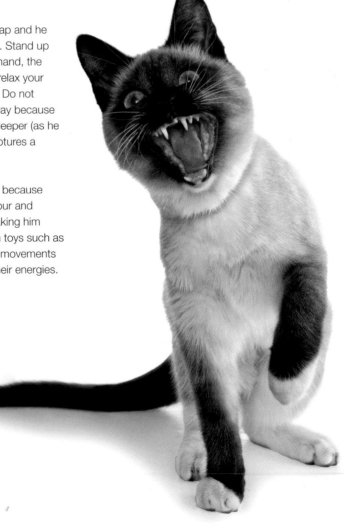

Indoor cats who do not receive enough mental and physical stimulation can become bored and lethargic.

ANXIETY (STRESS)
WHAT TO LOOK FOR:

When faced with circumstances beyond their control (including a visit to the vet), anxious cats tend to hide, vocalise, and even hiss because they are fuelled by fright. Extremely anxious cats can suffer from inflammatory bowel syndrome or may try to calm themselves by overly licking and biting at their coats. Some cats can develop separation anxiety if their favourite person is gone from home for long periods at a time.

HOW TO RESPOND:

Avoid talking in cooing tones or baby talk, as these vocalisations may cause your cat to feel more nervous and anxious. Cultivate a safe routine for your cat by teaching him to sit and stay in a spot and rewarding him with a healthy treat and gentle affection. Introduce him to a window perch where he can safely view the outside. Give your cat plenty of time to acclimatise to new family members or changes in the household routine.

In extreme cases, a vet may temporarily prescribe anti-anxiety medication coupled with behaviour modification designed to make your cat feel more at ease in the home environment.

BOREDOM
WHAT TO LOOK FOR:

Under-stimulated cats will sleep more than usual, may start overly grooming their coats, and may beg for more food. The root of the problem is that these cats lack an enriching indoor environment. Imagine being stuck in your house with no TV, no computer, no phone and no board games. Bored cats often spend long hours at home alone without cat furniture. In time, cats without stimulus can become physically depressed.

HOW TO RESPOND:

Jazz up your cat's indoor environment by positioning a comfy cat window perch in view of a bird or squirrel feeder hanging on a tree branch. Treat your cat to a tall cat-furniture tree in your living room, or a place where the family spends a lot of time. Offer your cat a couple of plant pots containing catnip or cat grass to munch on (see page 172 for plants to avoid).

Spend at least 10 minutes a day playing interactive games with your cat and rotate various cat toys each week to maintain his interest. When leaving the house, you might prefer to keep a radio or television switched on so the environment is not too quiet for your stay-home cat.

CURIOSITY
WHAT TO LOOK FOR:

Adventure-seeking cats sometimes put themselves in harm's way in their determination to investigate the surroundings. These cats boldly explore what is around them by tapping into all of their senses. The saying 'curiosity killed the cat' conveys the dangers awaiting a feline who risks physical injury by being a daredevil.

HOW TO RESPOND:

Definitely go room by room and pet proof your home to minimise the risk of injury toward your curious cat. That means putting sharp objects like scissors and sewing needles out of paw's reach, stabilising shelves, and keeping your cat out of the kitchen when you are cooking on a hot stove. Provide your curious cat with safe alternatives, such as battery-operated cat toys that feature a toy mouse spinning inside, for them to stalk and pounce upon.

Cats are quite capable of displaying a wide range of emotions, from feeling anxious to feeling playful to feeling downright angry.

OBSESSIVE-COMPULSION
WHAT TO LOOK FOR:

Cats with this behavioural disorder may pace, howl repetitively, over-groom their coats to the point of creating bald spots, repeatedly circle in attempts to catch their tails, or suck on wool clothing or plastic bags. Some cats progress to a medical condition known as feline hyperesthesia, characterised by rippling skin activity along the muscles of the back.

HOW TO RESPOND:

Identify causes of environmental stress within your home by going room to room. Did you relocate furniture? Welcome a new other member to the family (person or pet)? Your goal is to break these bad habits by providing your cat with a predictable daily routine for feeding, playing and socialising. Interrupt your cat when he starts to suckle on wool or begins to chase his tail. In some cases, your vet may need to prescribe behaviour-modification medications.

PLAYFULNESS (ATTENTION-SEEKING)
WHAT TO LOOK FOR:

Young, frisky kittens don't have a monopoly on play. Some senior cats maintain their zest for swatting toy mice, climbing up cat-tree furniture, and racing up and down hallways or stairs. Play-seeking felines may try to engage you by flopping on their sides and going belly-up, or pawing your arm or leg. They may engage you in catty conversations. Some overly zealous playful cats can bite people during play.

HOW TO RESPOND:

First, embrace this spirited feline who regards you as a prime playmate. Play-minded cats need and deserve mental and physical stimulation every day. Read out loud from your favourite book – these cats don't care about any story plotline, they just want your attention. These types are perfect candidates to learn cool cat tricks, such as sit, give me paw and sit up. Consider using clicker training when teaching your cat new tricks, and dish up lots of praise as these cats thrive on applause.

To properly interpret your cat's emotional state, you need to look at all of his body, heed any verbal cues, and take into account the situation in his environment.

Check out the crouched position and the focused eyes. This cat is on the prowl for a toy mouse.

PREDATORY
WHAT TO LOOK FOR:

A hyped-up hunter is a cat focused on stalking, chasing and pouncing on perceived prey. That prey can be a toy mouse or even your ankles. These cats tend to wait behind furniture or around a corner for the opportunity to strike. With flattened ears, tense bodies and twitching tails, they crouch low before attacking. These cats like to show off their hunting skills by depositing their conquests (dead mice or birds) on your pillow.

HOW TO RESPOND:

Offer a suitable hunting experience by occasionally going bowl-less at mealtime. Instead of filling the bowl with kibble, encourage your prey-minded feline to hunt for his pieces of food you strategically place in a room. Treat them to battery-operated cat toys (with flying faux birds or scampering toy mice) that move erratically for them to stalk and swat.

Shapes and Sounds

Genetics and life experiences certainly mould how cats think and act but other tools such as the shape of a cat's face, as well as the range of movements of a feline tail and types of miaow, offer an interesting insight.

If you plan to adopt a mixed-breed cat, how can you predict if he will be outgoing or reserved? In this section, we identify some possible personality predictors.

Cat Face Geometry

Some animal behaviourists contend that the physical facial shape may influence a cat's personality. Cat face geometry is an interesting technique that is being used at animal shelters to predict the personality characteristics in mixed-breed kittens or cats to help them finding loving, permanent homes. This theorises that certain personality clues may be linked to the shape of a cat's face. There are three types of face shape:

ROUND

Felines with circular heads, large eyes, flat faces and rounded bodies tend to be shy, gentle, prefer quiet homes, and are easily startled or frightened.

SQUARE

Cats with big, square-shaped faces and solid, large bodies tend to be outwardly affectionate, welcome guests, and love to snuggle. They are mellow and not easily rattled.

TRIANGLE

Cats with this geometric face shape sport big ears, faces that narrow at the nose, and long, lanky bodies. These cats tend to be very athletic, vocal, curious, and thrive in active households.

The grey cat depicted here sports a round face. It could be an indicator that this cat may be shy and is best suited in quiet homes.

The Tail Barometer

The tail serves a multitude of purposes, from providing balance to conveying moods. You can improve communication by responding to six specific 'tail talking' positions.

1 QUESTION MARK

This tail is bent in a question mark shape and signals that your cat is ready for playtime with you.

2 HOISTED HIGH

A tail erected like a flagpole flapping in the wind conveys a confident, contented cat.

3 PUFFED UP

A scared cat may try to bluff his perceived threat by making his tail expand to look like a pipe cleaner.

4 SWISHING

The tail that moves slowly from one side to the other occurs when a predatory cat is focused on his prey. The tail swishing occurs right before the pounce.

5 WHIPPING

Heed this feline warning. A cat who whips his tail quickly back and forth is agitated and clearly cautioning you to 'back off'.

6 TUCKED UNDER

Scared or submissive cats convey their nervousness and uncertainty by positioning their tails beneath their bodies.

The Miaow Scale

Cats can make a wide range of vocalisations and we don't always pay attention to them. Some cats are certainly chattier than others – they have a lot to discuss with their favourite people. Here are the most common feline sounds:

MIAOW

This two-syllable demanding tone is not one to ignore. A cat tired of being petted may sound this long, urgent vocalisation and may nip or swat if you don't cease petting him. Cats miaow loudly and repetitively if you forget to feed them on time.

MEW

This is a pleasing, short, high-pitched sound to attempt to get you to do something your cat wants, such as a second helping in the food bowl or toss the paper wad down the hallway…again. Kittens mew to their mothers when they want to nurse.

HISS

This elongated s-emphasising sound is an early warning that your cat is furious and unless you back off, he is prepared to bite or swat. Often, the cat displays a cold stare as well.

YOWL

Think of this as the feline equivalent of the human scream. Cats emit this screeching sound during a cat fight and some intact females yowl in heat in attempts to lure available males for mating.

CHIRP

Emitting from the throat, this musical trill features a question mark inflection at the end. Cats chirp as a friendly hello to humans and nursing mother cats chirp to alert the litter that it is time to nurse.

CACKLE

Indoor cats unable to reach a bird on a nearby tree branch do their best imitations of birds by making this 'ka-ka-ka' noise. Their lower jaw actually quivers as they cackle as they become highly aroused and frustrated at their inability to reach this flying prey.

HOW SMART IS YOUR CAT?

Cats are smart in their own way. Intelligence tests have been performed on pets with animal behaviourists equating the intellect of cats to the equivalent of a human toddler.

Here's a fun test designed to test your cat's IQ:

1. Pick a room free of any distractions. Usher other pets away and turn off the television so your cat can focus fully on you.

2. With your cat facing you, show him a small object you know he likes, such as a toy mouse. Make sure he sees it.

3. Hide this object behind something solid. You can use a folder or large book. Make sure your cat sees you doing this.

4. Time how long it takes for your cat to approach and look behind the solid object to find the toy or paper wad.

EXPLANATION: Super-smart cats have the cognitive development to know to look behind the solid object to find the 'missing' toy mouse or paper wad. Smart cats see a mouse or lizard scamper under a sofa. They have the intelligence to lay in wait for that prey to reappear so that they can pounce on it. Less smart cats leave the scene, perhaps subscribing to the mindset that 'out of sight is out of mind'.

There are ways to test if you share your home with an Einstein cat or one who is more sweet than smart.

Popular Breeds

Here is an inside look at the five most popular cat breeds – although do remember that every cat has its own special charm.

According to the international registry association, there are about 40 distinct cat breeds ranging in size from 2 kg to 9 kg (4–20 lbs) plus, and from nearly hairless to sporting a full, fluffy coat. Year after year, here are arguably the top five breeds in terms of popularity in ascending order:

Although recognised dog breeds outnumber cat breeds by a 3-to-1 margin, felines do come in a variety of looks, colours and temperaments.

1 ABYSSINIAN
APPEARANCE:

Long, lean and muscular, this breed has almond-shaped eyes, an arched neck, and oversized ears. The Abyssinian's coat feels like rabbit fur and comes in blue, fawn, red and ruddy colours.

BRIEF HISTORY:

This ancient breed hails from Egypt and images of the Abyssinian have been depicted in ancient Egyptian paintings and sculptures. The first Abyssinian arrived on North American soil from Great Britain in the early 1900s.

PERSONALITY:

The Abyssinian gets a capital 'A' for active. This cat thrives on mastering tricks and seeks out human audiences. The Abyssinian is also friendly and fearless.

PRIZE FACT:
The Abyssinian is nicknamed 'the bunny cat'.

2 SIAMESE
APPEARANCE:

This breed sports deep blue, almond-shaped eyes, a sleek, slender, muscular body, and regal-looking triangular-shaped head with large, pointed ears.

BRIEF HISTORY:

Siamese cats originated in Thailand, once known as Siam, and migrated to other parts of the world in the late 1800s.

PERSONALITY:

This is anything but a shy cat. Vocal, smart, outgoing and athletic, the Siamese demands interaction with his favourite people and his voice mimics the sound of a human baby.

🏵 PRIZE FACT:

According to feline folklore, the Siamese originated from a love match between a lioness and an ape aboard Noah's ark.

3 EXOTIC
APPEARANCE:

Sporting a thick, tangle-free coat and a round face, the Exotic is often viewed as a cross between a teddy bear and the Persian cat. Their coats come in bicolour, brown tabby, red tabby, tortoiseshell and black hues.

BRIEF HISTORY:

This breed was carefully created by professional American Shorthair breeders who mated their cats with Persians to produce this shorthaired cat with a Persian-like face.

PERSONALITY:

In their own quiet but determined way, Exotics sweetly seek out your attention and affection. Exotics are playful and easygoing.

🏵 PRIZE FACT:

The Exotic is also known as 'the lazy man's Persian' due to his easy-to-groom coat.

4 MAINE COON

APPEARANCE:

Towering over most cat breeds and weighing in at 6 kg (13 lbs) plus, the Maine Coon sports a waterproof, shaggy coat and tufts on his ears and toes to protect against harsh winters. The head is square in shape and broad with big, wide-set expressive eyes.

BRIEF HISTORY:

This all-American breed originated in the state of Maine and hails as the only indigenous breed of domestic cat from the United States.

PERSONALITY:

This is the perfect cat for households with kids and dogs as the Maine Coon is super mellow and tolerant. He is also very smart and affectionate and emits chirps and trills when contented.

Before selecting a specific breed of cat, do a candid self-assessment. Know how much time and energy you can devote to your cat and do not choose strictly by a cat's looks.

PRIZE FACT:

The Maine Coon has earned the nicknames 'Gentle Giant' and 'Feline Greeter of the World'.

5 PERSIAN

APPEARANCE:

With their trademark cherubic faces, expressive round eyes, and a soft, flowing, longhaired coat, the Persian has perennially reigned at the top among all feline breeds. His stocky body and heavy-boned legs are in contrast to his tiny, round-tipped ears.

BRIEF HISTORY:

This breed's origins remain inconclusive. Some believe this breed hails from Persia (now Iran), Russia and China, but others argue evidence of the Persian in ancient Egyptian hieroglyphics.

PERSONALITY:

Meet the feline couch potato. The Persian prefers lounging in quiet households and craves set routines.

🏵 PRIZE FACT:

The Persian was selected as the champion breed at the first modern cat show held at London's Crystal Palace in 1871.

CHAPTER 3

Grooming and Hygiene

Why Groom?

Cats reap numerous health dividends when you step in on occasion to brush their coats, trim their nails, brush their teeth and yes, even give them a bath.

 Although felines sport stellar reputations for being fastidious self-groomers, they definitely benefit from your assistance. There are good reasons to become your cat's personal groomer.

- Your cat is less apt to contend with matted coats or hairballs.
- You will be able to detect the presence of fleas, which can transmit disease such as tapeworms.
- You can find suspicious rashes, lumps, bumps and other skin-related conditions at the onset, and subsequently make a possible saving on veterinary bills.
- Your cat's claws won't become overgrown, causing them to snag or get stuck in the carpet.
- Your cat's breath will be fresh and her gums will be a healthy pink colour.

ESTABLISHING TRUST

Whether you are combing, bathing, or brushing your cat's teeth, remember to pet and talk to her. Rub her cheeks so that she gets her scent on your hands. From start to finish, sweet talk to keep her calm – avoid making any sounds that may be viewed as hissing or growling. Safe grooming sessions bolster the trust between your cat and you.

Your Cat's Coat

 No matter the breed or coat length, it's a sure bet that your feline's discarded hair will end up on your sofa, carpet, clothing and, on occasion, unluckily land in your coffee mug. But by investing in as little as 3 minutes of brushing and combing a day for shorthaired felines – and up to 8 minutes for longhaired felines – you can tame those manes and keep your home from looking like it got hit by a hairy tornado. Indoor cats especially need your help. Without exposure to a steady breeze, the coats of indoor cats are regularly exposed to household dirt and dust. When they self-groom, they ingest this extra dirt and dust.

A cat's coat is light sensitive, too. The more daylight exposed to the coat, the more it will shed. Indoor cats who crave the sunlight pouring in from a window, or those who sit under lights in the home, shed much more than outdoor cats. All cats shed – even so-called hairless breeds like the Sphynx. Surprisingly, longhaired breeds, such as the Persians and Norwegian Forest Cat, tend to shed less than shorthaired breeds such as the Abyssinian or Burmese. That's because longhaired cats are genetically programmed to have their hair fall out less often.

Help for Hairballs

The sad reality is that cats normally swallow hair when they groom. The tiny barbs on their tongue act like a hairbrush, grabbing loose hair. Most of the time, this swallowed hair passes through the digestive system without incident. However, when cats have a lot of hair to begin with or are shedding, swallowed hair accumulates in the stomach, where it can irritate the stomach lining and interfere with digestion. Once the hairball reaches a certain size, the cat vomits to expel a messy wad of hair, digested food, saliva and gastric secretions – the ingredients of your typical feline hairball.

HOME HAIRBALL REMEDY

The scientific name for hairball is trichobezoar. Any way you spell it, it is still a yucky mess and best rid of. Reach for the mineral oil, which acts like a safe and very effective lubricant to help your cat get rid of unwanted hairballs. Just add 1 teaspoon of mineral oil per 2.25 kg (5 lbs) of your cat's body weight to her food once or twice a week. So, if your cat weighs 4.5 kg (10 lbs), for example, add 2 teaspoons of mineral oil into her food.

Please consult your vet if the number of hairball incidents increases or if your cat appears to be in discomfort when she vomits. A radiograph may be necessary to determine if a hairball is stuck in her stomach. In some cases, impacted hairballs must be surgically removed.

Fortunately, you can reduce the hairball incidents by brushing and combing your cat daily. Another way to combat hairballs is to feed your cat a petroleum-based lubricant, available from your veterinary clinic or at most pet shops. Some cats tolerate straight Vaseline, but many don't like the taste. Whichever brand you use, dab a bit on your cat's nose or paw. She will automatically lick that area and ingest the lubricant. Most of these are flavoured to encourage cats to view them as a treat. Do not use butter or vegetable oil as they are high in calories and not absorbed efficiently by cats. Virgin olive oil can be used sparingly.

The overall health of your cat's coat, ears, eyes and mouth does ultimately depend on you – and how much time you are willing to devote to keeping her looking her very best.

Hair Care

Most cats rarely endure a bad hair day, but they make a mighty time investment – spending about one-third of their waking hours fussing over their coats. Although cats were born to groom, you can make a healthy difference by brushing them regularly.

Start off on the right 'paw' by selecting the right grooming tool for your cat. Depending on the breed, a cat's hair length ranges from less than 25–125 mm (1 in to 5 in).

SHORT HAIR

For shorthaired cats, your best grooming tools include the soft slicker brush with short, stiff bristles bunched closely together on a flat rectangular platform or a fine-toothed stainless steel comb.

LONG HAIR

For longhaired cats, rely on a soft slicker brush with long bristles widely spaced on a flat rectangular platform or a wide-toothed stainless steel comb – ideally, one with Teflon-coated teeth that glide easily through a cat's longhaired coat.

Don't forget to keep up your grooming regime on so-called 'hairless' cat breeds like Sphynx. Their coats are oily and need regular maintenance as well.

Grooming Guidance

When the time comes to groom, it is important that you heed these tips and tricks if you don't want to rub your cat up the wrong way.

1 PICK THE RIGHT ROOM.

Usher your cat to a small, confined room – ideally a bathroom – and close the door to prevent her from bolting out during the middle of the brush session. Save time on clean-up by keeping a plastic bag within reach to deposit the discarded hair retrieved from each stroke of the comb or brush.

2 KEEP SESSIONS SHORT.

A cat's skin is thinner than a dog's skin – and much thinner than a human's skin. Never comb one spot for 1 minute or longer, because it can cause that area to become bald and you'll end up stripping out the good fur with the loose, dead hair.

3 GROOM IN THE DIRECTION OF THE HAIR.

Always brush or comb in the direction that the fur grows: from the back of the head to the tail. For the hips and shoulders, the hair grows straight down, so brush or comb downwards. The hair on the tail grows sideways at a 90° angle, so always brush or comb the tail outwards at an angle from the base.

4 USE GLOVES.

One-size-fits-all grooming gloves quickly remove dirt, dust and dead hair from your cat's coat and are terrific for inbetween longer grooming sessions and when you want to have your cat look smart for guests. Or for quick grooming solutions, rub your cat's coat with pet wipes that reduce dander. Select brands that contain aloe vera or vitamin E to keep your feline's coat soft and shiny.

PREVENTING MATTED HAIR

Conquer knots in longhaired coats by brushing them daily, using a wide-toothed comb. Start by carefully pulling apart the matted hair with your fingers as much as you can or use a matt-splitter. Holding the matted hair at the base, gently but firmly brush out the mess with the comb by starting at the tip and working in towards the base. Do not use scissors to cut the knot because you risk accidentally cutting your cat's skin.

Sprinkling cornstarch on knots also helps to loosen the hair. Finish the grooming session by rubbing your cat's coat with a soft chamois cloth to add lustre.

For any knots you cannot comb out on your own, please seek help from a professional cat groomer.

---

5 USE BALLOONS TO PICK UP LEFTOVER HAIR.

Try rubbing an inflated balloon over upholstery to create static electricity. This should cause the short spiky pet hairs to pop up, therefore making it easier to vacuum them away.

6 TEST OUT CAT CLOTHES.

You don't have to create a new wardrobe just for your pet, but having your cat wear a pet jacket or jumper in the house can keep their excess hair under wraps – literally. Less hair will shed onto your bedspread or sofa. Just make sure that the indoor temperature is cool enough for your pet to sport her jacket.

Bath Time

Bathing your cat on occasion is a win-win for both you and your cat. Although don't expect her to purr with delight as she is lowered into a tub of warm, soapy water. This ceremony needs much practice.

Bathing helps combat skin problems and allergies for you and your pet. The excess hair coated with environmental allergy triggers, such as dust and pollen, goes down the drain – and not into your home. Avoid shampoos that contain artificial dyes, petrochemicals, parabens and sodium lauryl sulphate.

Bathing a cat helps rid her of grime, germs, dead skin and oils that have built up on her body – despite her daily grooming sessions. During the bath, you can clean the wax in her ears, gunk in her nails, tear staining around her eyes, and the dust layered on her legs from exiting the litter box several times a day. Follow this 10-step guide:

1 FAKE THE BATH AT FIRST.
Acclimatise your cat by going through the motions of bathing her a few times, to get her familiar with the routine before adding water. Get used to handling your cat and taking her to the bathroom. Close the door, put her in the sink and 'dry' her with a towel.

2 PREP THE BATHING AREA BEFOREHAND.
Have all your bathing supplies available within hand's reach in your bathroom: three towels (two for drying and one for her to grip), shampoo, brush, comb and treats. You don't want to be hunting for missing items once your cat is wet.

3 PICK THE RIGHT SHAMPOO.
Read the shampoo label carefully. Never bathe your cat in shampoo formulated for dogs because some ingredients in dog shampoos can be harmful to cats. Cats have more sensitive skin than dogs and it absorbs moisture faster. Most cats tend to have oily coats, so consider cat shampoos containing oatmeal and aloe.

4 DON'T USE THE BATH.
Opt for the bathroom sink or a large bucket. Many cats do not like running water, so set them up for success by using a bucket large enough to fit your cat and partially fill it with warm, soapy water. Put the cat's rear feet in the bucket first. Cats like something to grab onto so they can use their front paws to grab the top of the bucket, and always bathe them with the door closed to prevent escapes. Lightly turn on the water to get her used to hearing it before rinsing.

5 TEMPER THE WATER TEMPERATURE.
Use lukewarm water from a gentle spray nozzle, if possible. The water should be a soft spray against the cat's body and feel inviting, like a warm massage. Gradually wet your cat, starting from the bottom up. Never spray water up in the nose or inside the ears.

6 AVOID SOAP IN YOUR CAT'S EYES.
Never use a spray nozzle to wet your cat's face. Instead, clean the face with a warm, damp washcloth with a dab of shampoo. If you do get soap accidentally in your cat's eyes, repeatedly rinse out or, before the bath, take a little mineral oil and drop it in your cat's eyes to help protect them from soap.

GO WATER-FREE

For some elderly cats who may not be keen about bathtime, you have the option to make an appointment with a professional pet groomer or use waterless shampoo.

Select a water-free shampoo that is recommended by your vet. It should be free of any fragrances and definitely hypoallergenic. Consider waterless shampoos that come in dispensers filled with pre-moistened towelettes that you can glide down your cat's body. Or make this homemade dry shampoo remedy: Sprinkle a little bicarbonate of soda across your cat's back. Then use your fingertips in a circular motion to rub the powder deep into your cat's coat so that it reaches her skin. Repeat this every so often.

7 DON'T USE COTTON BUDS INSIDE EARS.

Avoid probing inside your cat's ears with cotton buds because of the risk of accidentally poking and damaging the eardrum. Use cotton balls to clean inside the ears, but don't probe deeper than what you can see easily.

8 RINSE OFF THE SHAMPOO THOROUGHLY.

If you do not rinse completely, your cat can end up with skin issues. She may start to chew her coat and develop skin irritations. One way to tell if you have rinsed thoroughly is to bring your ear down to the coat and squeeze the wet hair. If you hear a squeaky clean sound, that means you have rinsed out all the shampoo.

9 BE GENTLE WITH A HANDHELD BLOW-DRYER.

Have two thick bath towels within reach. Towel dry your cat well with the first towel, then snugly wrap your cat in the second towel and hold her closely. Speak sweetly to her to help her feel calm and secure. If you do use a hair dryer, brush the coat first and then only use the dryer at a low setting from a distance to avoid burning your cat's skin and causing painful scarring.

10 PICK A TIME WHEN YOU HAVE TIME.

Never attempt to groom or bathe your cat when you are in a hurry or your cat is agitated. You risk escalating her stress level and upping her resistance. Make these at-home bathing sessions inviting for your cat and teach her that everything is okay.

Nail Care

Cats rely on their claws to scent mark, grip and defend themselves.
That is why it is vital to keep your cat's nails healthy and trimmed.

Cats typically have five nails on each front paw and four nails on each back paw. These claws are curved and pointed and require the tips to be clipped every 2 weeks or so to prevent them from overgrowing and, worse, growing back into the paw.

Cats like to keep their nails sharp by scratching up and down, across and at an angle. Be sure to select a sturdy scratching post that offers these three surfaces.

Claw Clipping Guide

 Follow these quick and easy steps to help you give your feline a 'pet-icure'.

1 Make nail-trimming time fun. Before your first nail session, play with your cat's feet regularly to get her used to you touching her toes. Gently squeeze her footpads to expose the nails and release. Pet her and give her a small healthy treat.

2 Set out the tools you need: nail clippers designed for cats, a thick towel, and styptic powder (just in case you clip the nail too short and it bleeds).

3 Wrap your cat in a large bath towel, exposing one nail at a time to better handle her safely.

4 Position your thumb on top of one paw and your fingers of that hand underneath. Then gently press to expose the nail.

5 Snip the tip of the nail – the clear, white part. Do not cut too closely to the pink area of the nail called the quick – the vein that runs through the nail – or it will bleed.

6 Keep styptic powder or cornflour within reach just in case you do nick the quick, so you can then apply it fast in order to stop the bleeding.

7 Heap on praise during the trim session. You want your cat to have a positive experience.

8 Allow your cat to dash out the door before you. After opening the door for your cat to exit, purposely count to 10 before you leave and if possible, exit in the opposite direction that your cat took. This trick is to convey to your cat that nail-trimming time is no cause for panic.

SOFT CLAWS

A simple solution to persistent scratching and snags is to use Soft Claws or nail caps. These are made from nontoxic vinyl and are stuck using adhesive to trimmed cat claws. They do not interfere with the normal extension and retraction of your cat's claws and will fall off as the nail grows, lasting for approximately 4 to 6 weeks. Soft Claws come in a variety of sizes and colours, including transparent.

Teeth and Gum Care

One of the best ways to save on your veterinary bills is by keeping your cat's teeth and gums healthy by regularly performing at-home dental maintenance care.

It goes without saying that you love your cat and want her to be healthy and happy. But by age 3, nearly 75 per cent of cats develop some form of dental disease. The message is clear: cats, just like people, can develop gum disease, plaque and calculus buildup, oral tumours, and even need tooth extractions. Don't let your cat fall victim to periodontal disease. Maintain twice-a-year health examinations at your veterinary clinic as well as conducting these routine checks:

LOOK AND SNIFF.

Examine your cat's mouth daily. Report any swellings, bleeding or sores to your vet promptly.

MONITOR MEALTIMES.

Cats who eat slower than usual, suddenly spill kibble on the floor or back away from the bowl may be experiencing oral pain.

SHOP SMARTLY.

Select dental toys, treats, brushes and toothpastes that carry the VOHC seal of acceptance. That stands for Veterinary Oral Health Council – veterinary dentists who evaluate dental items and determine products that meet their approval. Look for the white tooth with a green sash for easily identifying VOHC-approved dental products. Cat toothpaste should contain antimicrobial enzymes and come in a flavour your cat likes, such as chicken, seafood or beef. Never use human toothpaste (contains fluoride) or dog toothpastes.

DAILY BRUSHINGS.

Treat your cat to good health by brushing their teeth with a toothbrush every day. Establishing a routine soon after you adopt your cat will be beneficial in the long run.

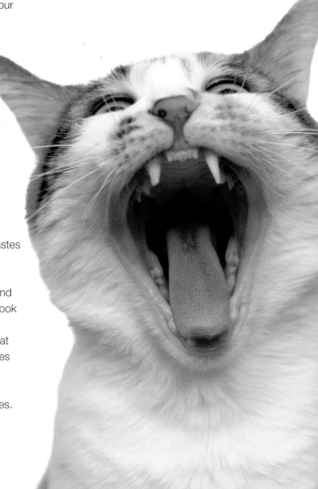

Toothbrushing Guide

Angled toothbrushes with soft angled bristles make it easier to brush the exterior on either side of the mouth. Finger toothbrushes feature soft bristles and enable you to slide it easily between your cat's gums and cheek.

There are a few toothbrushing position options available. Try placing your cat on a counter, or get down on the floor with your cat, or simply have your cat sit on your lap. With any of these, you will be able to reach your arm around and approach her mouth from the side. In other words, you won't face her head on, pushing a toothbrush straight into her mouth. Once you are in position, follow these recommended steps:

1 MASSAGE AND RUB YOUR CAT'S CHEEKS.

The idea is to get her used to you touching her face. Reward her with a small tasty treat. Do this briefly each day over several days or longer until your cat is comfortable with it.

2 INTRODUCE THE TASTE OF TOOTHPASTE.

Place some toothpaste on the toothbrush and let your cat lick it off.

3 HOLD YOUR CAT'S HEAD IN YOUR LESS-DOMINANT HAND.

Lift the cat's upper lip with the same hand. Use your dominant hand to massage your cat's cheeks briefly and then slip a finger into her mouth, just a little. Give her a treat. Repeat this daily.

4 STRIVE FOR GAINING YOUR CAT'S TRUST.

As tolerance builds up in succeeding daily sessions, gently use your finger to rub back and forth over the gum line. Start at the front of the mouth, and then move to the back upper and lower gum areas. The idea is to get your cat accustomed to having something in the mouth. Reward with a treat.

5 UP THE ANTE.

Now that your cat accepts a finger in her mouth, you're ready to begin the hygiene session. Wrap gauze around your finger. With a circular motion, rub your cat's teeth and gums along the gum line. Try to apply some digital pressure to the teeth and gums. Usually, there is no need to open the cat's mouth into a gape – plaque is mostly accumulated on the cheek surfaces of the teeth. Reward with a treat. Repeat over the course of days or weeks until she accepts this routine.

6 TIME FOR THE TOOTHBRUSH.

Hold the toothbrush at a 45° angle to the gum line. Move your choice of toothbrush with an oval motion or brush back and forth. Start with the outer surfaces and possibly finish with the inner surfaces. That way, if your cat gets fed up, the most likely areas of plaque accumulation have been brushed. Keep the session brief – just a minute or two. Reward with a treat.

ALTERNATIVE OPTIONS

If your cat won't tolerate you brushing her teeth, use oral rinses, oral cleansing gels, dental gauze, water additives you add into your cat's water bowl, and dental treats instead. Top-quality dental products feature antibacterial and odour-fighting properties.

CHAPTER 4
Food and Nutrition

Mealtime Measures

What goes in the food bowl plays a key role in the longevity and health of cats. But bringing out the nutritional best in your cat goes beyond what's served in the bowl.

Cats crave and need quality proteins. They can do well on grains, but not on all-grain diets because they don't metabolise as quickly to absorb the glucose as people do. Frequency of meal feedings, location, post-meal bowl cleaning and other environmental issues can also influence the health of your cat. To make mealtime more satisfying and safe, factor in these environmental considerations:

PROVIDE MINI-MEALS RATHER THAN ONE BIG MEAL.

In general, cats are grazers. Small mini-meals, say in the morning, when you come home from work, and right before bedtime can also help maximise your cat's metabolism.

USE MEASURING CUPS AND SPOONS.

Although suggested food portions are often put on the bags of commercial dry food and tinned foods, measure your cat's meals precisely and work with your vet on establishing the right daily portions that meet your cat's age, health condition, and activity level. By knowing how much you are feeding, the portion can be adjusted if your vet determines you are under- or overfeeding your cat.

SEPARATE CATS AT MEALTIMES.

If you have more than one cat, this is especially important if you have a feline food bully or a cat on a therapeutic diet. Mealtimes should be calm, welcoming events so that cats can properly digest their food. Cats in the household trying to steal another cat's food can cause stress and possibly,

even gastrointestinal upset. Vets recommend training the cats to eat in separate rooms at mealtimes, where doors can be closed. Cats like routine and, in time, they may even park themselves in front of their designated rooms at mealtime waiting for you to feed them.

CLEAN FOOD AND WATER BOWLS.

Food bowls can be coated with salmonella in the bio-film. Water in bowls can get stale. Thoroughly clean your cat's bowls after each meal in hot soapy water and rinse thoroughly and allow to air dry. And, don't forget to regularly clean your pet's measuring cup or serving scooper.

RESIST BUYING GIGANTIC BAGS OF FOOD.

You will get more than you bargained for if you buy in bulk because there is an increased risk of the food becoming stale and contaminated. Instead, buy about 1 month's worth of dry food and empty the food into a plastic container with a lid. Before refilling that container, always thoroughly clean it and allow it to air dry because fats sprayed on the dry food leave a greasy film on the inside walls of the container, which can cause the new food to quickly become rancid.

PAY HEED TO THE CONTENTS OF YOUR FLOOR-CLEANING PRODUCTS.

Many household cleaning products contain bleach effective in killing viruses on the kitchen floor. Cats have sensitive noses and some may be repelled by the odour of cleaners, so never clean your kitchen floors before mealtimes.

WATER INTAKE

It can be challenging to make sure your cat laps up enough water each day to stay properly hydrated. Far too many cats do not drink enough water and are at risk for being dehydrated. You can't 'command' a cat to head to the water bowl.

But here are tips and tricks to increase your cat's water intake:

- Serve up tinned food. Canned food contains more moisture than any commercial dry food.
- Add sodium-free broth to your cat's dry food to make it more appealing to him.
- Locate water bowls throughout the house so your cat doesn't have far to travel to find a watery oasis.
- Add tuna juice to your cat's water to up the interest.
- Avoid letting your tap drip because you will incur a large water bill. Instead, provide a cat fountain that features moving water.

SELECT FOOD AND WATER BOWLS CAREFULLY.

The type of bowl you select to fill with food or water does matter to your cat's health. The healthiest bowls are made of stainless steel or ceramic. Both are easy to clean thoroughly. Avoid plastic bowls because they can be easily nicked or chewed and thus create hidden havens for salmonella or other bacteria, causing digestive upset in your feline friend. Some cats do not like having their whiskers scrunched when they eat from deep food bowls. Try replacing that bowl with a plate or wide, flat bowl.

Purchasing Food

Not all commercial cat food is created equally. Your feline friend must rely on you to be a smart consumer and select the best food to meet his nutritional needs.

Step into any pet shop, supermarket, or even inside veterinary clinics and you can quickly become overwhelmed by all the choices of commercial cat food available. Interpreting cat food labels can prove to be a daunting task. To help you crack the commercial pet food code, here are some tips:

WHAT TO LOOK FOR
WHOLE PROTEIN AS THE FIRST INGREDIENT.

The ingredients are listed in order of weight, with the first one being the heaviest. Since your cat is an obligate carnivore, look for commercial diets that contain any of these highly digestible proteins as the first ingredient: chicken, beef, salmon, lamb, turkey. Avoid products listing 'meat', 'poultry' or 'meat by-products' as the No. 1 ingredient. By-products can include feathers, feet, hooves, beaks and other unsavoury body parts used in the processing. Really pay attention to the first five ingredients – they represent the majority of the ingredients contained in the commercial food. Skip products that list maize or wheat as one of the first three ingredients.

MANUFACTURER TRANSPARENCY.

A quality commercial food manufacturer makes it easy for the consumer to contact them by listing their website, consumer hotline phone number and where their products are made. They will also include an expiration date.

PROOF THAT THE FOOD IS COMPLETE AND BALANCED.

The label should confirm that the product is formulated to meet the nutritional levels established by a pet food monitoring agency. If an over-the-counter food labels states 'for intermittent or supplemental use only', it is not complete and balanced and should not be fed on a permanent basis. Therapeutic diets prescribed by veterinary surgeons may have this phrase when they are used to help manage medical conditions, but these special diets should always be fed under the supervision of a vet.

A NUTRITIONAL LABEL FOR LIFE STAGES.

The life stages for felines include growth (kitten), adult maintenance, and reproduction (for pregnant and nursing mothers).

Try not to buy more than a month's worth of dry food. Store it in an airtight container to prevent it from becoming stale or contaminated.

WHAT TO AVOID
PACKAGING STATING 'HOLISTIC', 'LIGHT', 'PREMIUM' OR 'ALL-NATURAL'.

These are merely meaningless marketing terms designed to attract consumers and are not as the result of meeting any quality standard established within the pet food manufacturing industry or its monitoring agencies.

GRAIN-FREE COMMERCIAL DIETS ARE NOT ALWAYS FREE OF CARBOHYDRATES.

Even if the packaging claims to be 'grain-free', look at the list of ingredients. Some brands are loaded with carbohydrates like potatoes or maize.

ARTIFICIAL COLOURS, FLAVOURS, SUGARS AND CHEMICAL PRESERVATIVES (SUCH AS BHA AND BHT).

Your cat deserves to eat healthy, clean food and not ingest potentially dangerous preservatives or chemicals in his diet.

CHOOSING TINNED FOOD OVER DRY FOOD BASED ON PERCENTAGE OF PROTEIN LISTED.

Be aware that the protein percentage in tinned food is not on par with the protein percentage of dry food because canned food contains about 75 per cent moisture as compared to dry food which contains about 10 per cent moisture. Comparing protein content from tinned to dry can be confusing, so please ask your vet for help.

MANUFACTURER DAILY FEEDING RECOMMENDATIONS.

These recommendations are coming from the manufacturer and may be more than your cat needs. Instead, work with your vet to identify the right amount of food to feed your cat based on his age, health and activity level in order to keep him at a healthy weight.

Making Food

One way to a cat's heart is through his stomach. Show how much you love your cat once in a while by heading to the kitchen and taking on the role of feline chef.

 On special occasions, don an apron and treat your cat to a homemade nutritious meal. Here are three recipes that will evoke plenty of purrs. Bon appétit!

KITTY HASH
🥫 YOU WILL NEED:
1 cup water
½ cup uncooked brown rice
2 tsp corn oil
Pinch of salt
⅔ cup lean ground turkey
2 tbsp chopped raw beef or chicken liver
MAKES: *4 portions*

1 In a medium pan,
bring the water to a boil.

2 Stir in the rice, corn oil and salt and reduce
the heat to low. Cover the pan with a lid and
allow the mixture to simmer for 20 minutes.

3 Add the ground turkey and chopped liver to
the pan. Stir frequently and simmer for 20
more minutes.

4 Allow to cool before serving. Store in an
airtight container in your refrigerator.

TUNA PATTIES
🥫 YOU WILL NEED:
2 eggs
1 185 g can of tuna in springwater, drained
and flaked
1 cup breadcrumbs
1 tsp brewer's yeast
Pinch of salt
2 tbsp margarine
MAKES: *6 portions*

1 In a medium-sized bowl,
whisk the eggs.

2 Add the tuna, breadcrumbs, brewer's yeast
and salt. Blend with a wooden spoon until
moistened and thoroughly mixed.

3 Form the mixture
into 6 patties.

4 In a large frying pan, melt the margarine over
medium heat.

5 Place each of the patties into the frying pan.
Cook each side for 3 to 5 minutes or until
golden brown.

6 Allow the patties to cool and then crumble
them into small pieces.

7 Store in an airtight container
in your refrigerator.

(Substitute tuna with tinned salmon or white fish.)

TUNA ICE LOLLY
YOU WILL NEED:

1 185 g can of tuna in springwater
1 tsp organic catnip, crushed finely
MAKES: *1 tray of ice cubes*

1 Drain the liquid from the tuna into a pouring cup.

2 Fill a plastic ice cube tray halfway with bottled water.

3 Lightly sprinkle catnip into each of the cube holders in the tray.

4 Fill the rest of the ice cube tray with the tuna water.

5 Carefully store the tuna tray in your freezer.

6 Wait a few hours until the cubes are frozen solidly. Then, plop one tuna lolly into your cat's clean bowl and watch him enjoy this homemade fishy feast.

When you treat your cat to a homemade meal, make it extra special by serving it in a special dish.

HOME-COOKING HYGIENE

Keep your cat from stomach upset when making a homemade meal by always:

- Washing your hands in warm soapy water and rinsing well before handling food.
- Trimming meats of fat and draining excess grease from cooked meats.
- Storing leftovers in airtight containers in the refrigerator.

Treats

Your cat could be napping in a bedroom, but at the sound of a treat bag being opened or a treat jar being shaken, he is up, alert and now begging by your side. Did someone say treat?

When you come home, don't automatically give your cat a treat because you feel guilty that he was home all day while you were at work. In essence, you are merely replacing 'affection' with 'confection'. What your cat really wants is your attention. Bring out your cat's innate hunter by making him work for his food by placing a daily portion of his kibble in treat balls that require him to swat to cause the kibble to fall onto the ground. He will love the interaction with you and interaction is calorie free.

Don't go crazy on doling out the treats. The amount of treats should represent only 10 per cent of your cat's daily nutritional needs, or about 20 to 25 calories. Most cats maintain healthy weights when they consume between 200 and 250 calories of food per day. The majority of that food should be their regular kibble or canned cat food – not treats or table scraps.

Far too many people feel guilty that they live busy lives and don't have time to exercise their pets, so they show their love by doling out food and treats. Instead, engage your cat in a short play session while you treat.

Is Your Cat Crazy for Catnip?

One out of two cats craves catnip *(Nepeta cataria)*, the fragrant herb from the mint family. The plant's leaves contain an oil called nepetalactone, which evokes such feline antics as chin and cheek rubbing, rolling and kicking, and even leaping into the air. This oil closely resembles a substance present in a feline cat's urine. Strange but true!

In selecting this herb for your cat, opt for organic catnip in cat toys or to be sprinkled on their scratching posts. Organic catnip is the most potent. Always store this herb in an airtight container to keep it aromatic. Catnip's effects last between 3 and 15 minutes for most cats. About 70 per cent of cats exposed to catnip do display some type of reaction. Interestingly, kittens don't show any reaction until they are at least 6 weeks of age.

However, some felines turn their noses up at catnip. If you have such a cat, don't fret. Try honeysuckle-filled toys instead. Honeysuckle elicits a similar but less intense reaction than catnip for some cats. You must moisten the honeysuckle to activate its aroma.

CATNIP FOR YOU!

Got a frisky feline with a case of night-time crazies? Treat him to catnip at bedtime so he can unleash his energy and tire out. Then, make yourself a cup of freshly steeped catnip tea. It turns out that in people, catnip acts like a sedative, not a stimulant as it does in cats. By the time you finish sipping your tea, your cat will have finished racing around and both of you can drift off into dreamland.

Behold the magical catnip plant, which garners the interest of most adult cats and triggers kitten-like play in them.

Treats to Avoid

 Some cats are deemed finicky eaters while others are more enthusiastic eaters, quickly gobbling up any and all food opportunities. Unlike many dogs, who tend to eat first and think second, cats tend to be more selective in their cuisine choices. Keep in mind that the primary palatability motivators for cats are protein and fat content. And recognise that because your cat's body metabolises food differently from you, some foods – and medicines – deemed perfectly safe for you can be downright dangerous and deadly if eaten by your cat.

Veterinary nutritionists and toxicologists share this list of human foods and drinks to definitely never give to your cat:

RAW FISH OR MEAT

You may be a fan of the sushi bar at a Japanese restaurant, but don't give your cat any sushi leftovers or any uncooked fish or meat. Human-grade sushi is safe for people, but can cause gastrointestinal upset in cats. Left unrefrigerated, raw fish or meat can contain bacteria such as salmonella, which can cause vomiting and diarrhoea in your cat. In addition, an enzyme in raw fish can destroy an essential B vitamin called thiamine that cat's need.

UNCOOKED EGGS

Again, you risk exposing your cat to salmonella and other parasites that could cause vomiting, diarrhea, dehydration and, possibly, pancreatitis.

COOKED BONES

Never give a cat anything that is harder than their teeth because it can cause fractured teeth. Bones can splinter and block a cat's intestinal tract, causing choking or, worse, perforate the intestines.

FAT FROM MEATS

If you want your feline carnivore to enjoy a piece of your T-bone, cut a small lean piece and set it aside to give him as a reward for not begging. Do not give him the fat or gristle from the steak. The fat can cause vomiting, diarrhoea and inflammation of the pancreas, leading to pancreatitis.

MILK

This dairy drink lands on the cautionary list. An occasional small amount of milk may be okay to some cats, but keep in mind that a cat's digestive tract becomes somewhat lactose-intolerant after kittenhood. Daily servings of milk can cause diarrhoea and vomiting.

AVOCADOS

The biggest health danger to cats is the persin found in the plant, leaves and fruit itself. Ingestion can cause vomiting and diarrhoea in cats.

ONIONS, CHIVES AND GARLIC

Cats do not metabolise the alliums found in onions, chives and garlic as well as people do. These foods in any form (raw, powdered, cooked or dehydrated) can cause gastrointestinal upset and the destruction of red blood cells, leading to Heinz anaemia in some instances.

CAFFEINATED COFFEE, TEA AND SODA

Curious cats may be drawn to lapping up your caffeine-loaded drink, but too much caffeine consumption can cause restlessness, heart palpitations, rapid breathing, muscle tremors and, possibly, seizures in your feline.

MACADAMIA NUTS

You may want to spoil yourself with these tasty and pricey nuts, but be aware that a cat who eats these types of nuts can choke, suffer vomiting and diarrhoea and, in some cases, even paralysis.

SAFE FOODS

On occasion, it is okay to give your cat a little tinned tuna, a tiny piece of your steak or a small bit of cheese. But keep in mind that cats only need about 200 to 250 calories a day, so go easy on the portions.

UNCOOKED BREAD DOUGH

Your placement of dough on a baking sheet on your kitchen counter could spell an invitation to a food-seeking cat. Remember that the yeast in this dough rises. So, the dough can cause your cat's abdomen to swell and stretch, causing severe pain. It can even ferment and expand in your cat's stomach, causing signs similar to drunkenness.

ALCOHOL

It only takes a small amount – two teaspoons of whisky – to damage your cat's liver, put him in a coma, or kill him. So keep all beer, wine and hard liquor out of access to your cat. A cat can get drunk, nauseous, and his respiration can be affected. And, a cat can aspirate vomit in his lungs. A cat can also injure himself because the alcohol has left him uncoordinated.

CHOCOLATE

We know this sweet treat is a dangerous temptation to dogs. Fortunately, cats lack sweet taste receptors and therefore are not usually drawn to sugary foods, but there is always a feline exception. Ingesting the ingredient, theobromine, found in chocolate can cause high heart rate, high blood pressure, tremors and seizures in a cat. So keep your candies out of paw's reach.

Sizing Up Your Cat

Extra weight in cats hikes their risk for developing diabetes, respiratory and arthritic conditions. Sadly, these are often chronic, incurable, and generally preventable diseases.

Nearly half of the world's beloved pets are overweight or obese, and the root cause often starts at the food bowl. Is your cat too chubby to leap up on his cat tree? Curb greediness and shed excess pounds gradually but steadily off your cat.

TAKE BEFORE AND AFTER PHOTOS.
Help your cat slim down smartly by taking a 'before' photo of him and put this photo in a visible place such as on your refrigerator door. Start a food diary and weigh your cat once every week.

COUNT THE KIBBLE.
Feeding as little as 10 extra pieces of kibble per day would add 0.5 kg (1 lb) of weight in a year in your cat. So, use a measuring cup at mealtimes.

SET REALISTIC WEIGHT-LOSS GOALS.
It's best for a cat to lose only a few kilos per week so that the excess weight comes off gradually and doesn't return. Don't cut back too quickly. In cats, the dangers of 'crash dieting' can lead to hepatic lipidosis, more commonly known as fatty liver disease.

OPT FOR SCHEDULED FEEDINGS.
Instead of filling up your cat's bowl whenever it is empty, use a measuring cup and portion out your cat's daily meals twice a day. If you are unable to be home at a specific mealtime, consider buying a timed self-feeder that can dispense controlled portions of kibble at designated times.

CHAMPION TINNED FOOD.
Tinned food is what vets regard as a close-calorie environment because you know precisely how many calories are in a tin. Canned foods contains moisture, higher fat and protein, and are lower in carbohydrate than some dry foods.

STICK WITH SIMPLE FOOD CHOICES.
Look for treats with a single ingredient listed such as sweet potato, blueberry, salmon flakes, or dried beef lung. If the label's list of ingredients reads like a chemistry equation, avoid this product. These treats contain additives, preservatives and more calories.

ASK YOUR VETERINARY SURGEON QUESTIONS.

To keep tabs on your cat's health, ask your vet these questions: What should I feed my pet? How much should I feed my pet? How much exercise does my pet need? What types of exercises are best for my pet? What vaccines does my pet need and why?

ENCOURAGE YOUR CAT TO MOVE AND PLAY.

Try putting a low-calorie treat like shaved bonito fish flakes at the top of the stairs when your cat is at the bottom of the stairs. Show him the treat and call him up. Drag a toy on a string for him to chase. Basically, step up daily feline aerobics so your cat doesn't spend his day napping and not moving.

ASSESSING YOUR CAT

Not sure if your cat is sporting extra weight? Many cats have muffin tops' that may inaccurately make them appear to be hefty. You need to assess your cat by following these steps:

1 Stand in front of your standing cat. Exam his body profile. He should have a clearly defined abdomen slightly tucked up behind his rib cage.

2 Stand over your standing cat. Most cats have an hourglass shape and you should be able to see his waist.

3 Gently run your fingers over your cat's backbone and spread your hands over his rib cage. You should be able to feel each rib.

>))))● Now it is time to check your results. If your cat is obese, fat deposits are readily visible on the neck, limbs, base of tail and spine. If your cat is overweight, the waist is barely visible and you can see fat deposits over the lumbar area and base of the tail. You can feel the ribs, but just barely.

>))))● On a fit cat, you can feel the ribs without a lot of fat covering. Looking from the side, you can see the abdomen tucked up and you will see the hourglass shape when you look over your cat. If your cat is too thin then his ribs, pelvic bones and lumbar vertebrae protrude out and are highly visible.

>))))● Alternatively, there is another quick trick to determine if you have a fat cat. First, glide the fingers of one hand over the back of your other hand. Feel the bones? Now, take your hand and glide over the base of your cat's back near his tail. Healthy cats have that same bony feeling you identified in gliding your fingers over the back of your hand. Hefty cats have a fat cushion that can be detected.

CHAPTER 5
Behaviour Issues

Tackling Problem Behaviours

Cats make declarations. They see no harm in asking for what they want and can display 'tricky' behaviours to live with. In their view, the home belongs to them and, in reality, they are there much more than you are.

People often misunderstand felines. What might be considered a misdeed, such as shredding the arm of the sofa like confetti, to a cat is instead an opportunity to mark the home with her scent and telltale scratches to inform other felines that this is her domain. Cats, in fact, crave household routines and are not erratic. They need and deserve a lofty, stable perch inside the home to enable them to survey their surroundings from a safe height. They need and deserve litter boxes that are scooped daily and

positioned in a location away from barking dogs or other privacy invaders. This section identifies some feline behaviours that may puzzle, amuse or frustrate you – with tips and tricks designed to restore harmony in your household.

Ambushing Ankles
SCENARIO:

You walk down the hallway, turn the corner, and – ouch! – your feisty feline has been patiently lying in wait to pounce. When she hears or first sees you approaching, her back end elevates and she wiggles quickly side to side. Then she springs from her hiding spot and wraps her front claws around your ankle.

MOTIVATION:

Indoor cats need and deserve opportunities to hone their hunting skills. Their 'prey' is not the rodents or birds abundant in the great outdoors, but, anything that moves inside the home for her to stalk and attack. Your cat is simply redirecting the need for natural play towards you.

If you only have one cat, this behaviour could indicate that she feels deprived of sufficient playtime. She is desperately looking for ways to act out her play-prey aggression.

SOLUTIONS:

Try to ignore your cat during the attack and walk away. When your cat is calm, avoid overstimulation by limiting friendly pats and strokes to 10-second intervals and never engage in overly boisterous play.

Invest in interactive toys like wands with feathers or low-power, low-voltage laser lights made specifically for cats. Schedule 5 to 10 minutes twice a day to play with your cat.

Alternatively, outfox your pouncing cat. Walk down the hall and stop just before the door where your cat is hiding. Toss a favourite toy mouse or even a paper wad down the hall in the opposite direction you are heading. You want to elicit a play response in your cat. Your cat will be occupied with 'killing' this faux mouse to enable you to walk safely by. Do this each morning to introduce a safer, friendlier ritual and your feline should now lie in wait for the toy mouse, instead of your vulnerable ankles.

Or, consider getting her a feline playmate. Adopting another cat may provide her with a more suitable outlet for her stalking activities. Work with your local animal shelter on finding a perfect playmate match for your cat and you.

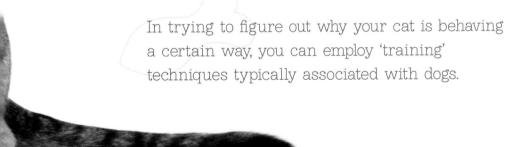

In trying to figure out why your cat is behaving a certain way, you can employ 'training' techniques typically associated with dogs.

Waking You Up
SCENARIO:

It is 2 hours before your alarm clock is set to sound. Then it happens. You are jarred awake by your wide-awake cat who pounces on your toes, purrs loudly in your ear, paws your nose, walks across your stomach, paws the window blinds, or starts knocking books off your bedside table.

MOTIVATION:

Before you get angry at the cat, blame yourself – especially if you have got into the habit of leaping out of bed when she rudely wakes you up, and dash to the kitchen to prepare a meal for her as a way to get her to quiet down and leave you alone. In your cat's mind, she is thinking mission accomplished. Cats like daily routines and your cat has discovered that if she wakes you up earlier each pre-dawn, she is 'rewarded' with breakfast.

SOLUTIONS:

If you want a good night's sleep, you need to reset your cat's inner clock. Start by changing her feeding schedule and serve her dinner later in the evening, ideally, before you head to bed, instead of when you first return home from work. A full belly will help her sleep longer; hopefully past dawn. The next step is to do your best to ignore your cat when she awakens you during this transitional phase. Without speaking a word to her, get out of bed, brush your teeth, check your email, or watch a bit of the morning news. Purposely wait 30 minutes to an hour before you prepare her breakfast after you wake up. Expect her to protest loudly at first but be as stubborn as a cat, and in time your cat will adjust to the new morning routine.

Behold the non-blinking stare down from a cat who insists on not letting you sleep in.

Using Houseplants Like a Toilet
SCENARIO:
You discover that your cat has opted to munch on leaves and deposit 'feline fertiliser' in the soil of potted plants rather than use her litter box. The odour can be overwhelming and your carpet littered with spilt dirt.

MOTIVATION:
Some cats like the feel of soft dirt to dig out a place to urinate or defecate. It may be her less-than-subtle signal to you that the litter box is not clean enough for her use and she is looking for alternative toileting options. Otherwise, the litter box may be too small or in a location she does not like – such as next to a noisy washing machine.

SOLUTIONS:
You can grow an indoor garden and keep your cat contented and out of the plants. For starters, layer the soil surfaces of the targeted plants with surfaces that are not appealing to cats, such as rough-edged decorative rock or prickly pinecones. You can also put double-sided sticky tape around the top of the pot to prevent your cat from hopping in. Next, hoist some of your favourite potted plants on ceiling hooks to keep them out of paw's reach. Finally, make the plants less tasty by spritzing them with citronella, vinegar, Tabasco sauce or bitter apple.

If your cat does enjoy nibbling on greens, treat her to a tray of cat grass (*Avena sativa*), also known as the common oat grass. It takes about a week to reach a good nibbling height.

Before adorning your interior with beautiful flowers, make sure the bouquet is not dangerous to your cat.

Leaving 'Gifts'
SCENARIO:

You come home to discover your cat sitting proudly at the top of the stairs next to a dead mouse. Or worse, you wake up to find that while you were sleeping a dead mouse has been deposited on your bedroom pillow. The 'gift' could also be a deceased rat, bird or other small prey.

MOTIVATION:

Cats can't grab the car keys and head to the florist shop or type on the keyboard and order a box of gourmet chocolates to convey their admiration for their favourite people. Depositing dead prey is their way of delivering presents to you. But it is also a sign that she views you as a lousy hunter and is attempting to hone your hunting skills. Mother cats train their kittens by first bringing a dead mouse to the litter for them to inspect. Then she brings a half-dead mouse and kills it in front of the kittens. Finally, she brings a live mouse to the kittens for them to demonstrate what she has taught them.

SOLUTIONS:

It may be hard to do, but resist screaming at the sight of your dead gift. Definitely do not scold your cat, either, as that will only cause feline confusion and harm your friendship connection. Instead, place a bell on her collar if she ventures outdoors, to warn the rodents of her approach. Also provide her with fake, safe prey to stalk and chase inside, such as a battery-operated toy mouse that makes erratic movements. Then sit back and applaud her agile, athletic performance.

Far Too Chatty
SCENARIO:

It seems like your cat's waking hours are filled with loud miaows and howls, often directed at you. She positions herself between you and your destination in the house and begins her one-sided passionate conversation.

MOTIVATION:

Some feline breeds were born talkers. The Siamese and Bengal top the chatty cat list as they sport reputations for demanding interaction with their favourite people. Cats tend to communicate more verbally with people – perhaps because we rely on the spoken word – than with other cats, by which they tend to communicate using body postures. Some smart cats are quick studies and realise that they can get what they want by vocalising their demands on us.

SOLUTIONS:

If only there was a mute button to push on a feline loudmouth! First, let's address what NOT to do: yelling at your yappy cat or tossing a pillow at her only 'rewards' her by giving her the attention she wants. Instead, you need to reward quiet behaviour. Give her friendly rubs on the cheeks or under her chin or give her a small healthy treat when she is sitting patient. Re-channel her chattiness by engaging her in learning new tricks, such as sit, shake paws, and other cues. Finally, be patient to change your cat to be less mouthy.

MEDICAL NOTE:

If your cat suddenly becomes highly vocal, that could be due to an underlying medical condition that warrants having her examined by your veterinary surgeon.

High-pitched miaows and loud yowls emitted by an insistent cat can quickly get on one's nerves. Work with your cat to change this behaviour.

Chewing and Sucking
SCENARIO:

You reach into your wardrobe shelf to fetch your favourite wool sweater only to discover that there is a baseball-sized hole in the middle of it. Or you drop a plastic shopping bag on the ground and your cat grabs it, takes it to the corner and begins vigorously licking the bag from top to bottom.

MOTIVATION:

Blame your cat's family tree and her super sense of smell for these two quirky behaviours. The eating of inedible items by cats has the scientific term 'pica'. Some breeds, particularly Siamese and Burmese, are genetically more prone to suck or chew on wool. Some behaviour experts theorise that the scent of lanolin in wool mimics the scent emitted from a mother cat's nipple. Or the food your cat eats lacks adequate fibre and she is searching for more. As for the plastic bag attraction, there is speculation among vets that cats crave the gelatin utilised during the manufacturing of some plastic bags because gelatin is an animal product and cats are meat eaters. Some cats simply like the coolness of the plastic bag and how the texture feels on their barbed tongues.

SOLUTIONS:

Your cat is forcing you to be a tidier housekeeper. Most wool-sucking cats outgrow this habit by age 3, so during her youth you need to keep wool clothing inside drawers or in wardrbobes with doors securely shut. Kiss goodbye the days where you could simply drop your dirty clothes in a pile on the floor – they need to be promptly dropped in a laundry basket with a lid. Stash plastic bags also out of reach of your cat.

Also consult your vet about ways to increase fibre in your cat's diet. When you catch her in the act of chewing and sucking, don't yell or punish her and instead offer her a toy to fetch or swat or treat her to a grooming session. Both of these tactics are designed to interrupt the sucking or chewing behaviour. Finally, make sure your cat isn't ingesting the wool or plastic as it can cause her to choke and possibly, stop breathing because the material is blocking her airway. In the latter case, you need to call for emergency veterinary attention.

On Kitchen Worktops
SCENARIO:

Just as your guests arrive for a dinner party, your cat is sauntering on your dining room table, sniffing at the party food and drink. Another more dangerous scenario is your cat exits the litter box and makes a beeline for your kitchen counter, which harbours feline dangers such as the paring knife, sliced onions and maybe a glass of wine.

MOTIVATION:

Cats like perching on high places. They enjoy being able to survey their surroundings from an elevated spot, which explains why some cats hang out on the top of refrigerators or even balance on the top of doors that are ajar. They also like to investigate tempting smells, which is why they conduct patrols multiple times a day on your kitchen worktops.

SOLUTIONS:

To break your cat of the habit of leaping on the dining room table or kitchen worktops, you need to temporarily make those surfaces anything but feline friendly. Stop your stubborn worktop climber by placing baking sheets on your table or counter. Add water to these sheets. Then the next time your cat leaps up, splash: her paws land in this unexpected lake. You can also place double-sided tape on the surfaces. Cats rely on their feet to mark their territories, so they like to keep them impeccably clean and, so, when a cat jumps on a sticky-coated counter, it will quickly become an unwelcome surface to her.

These feline 'booby trap' strategies work 24 hours a day, even when you are away from home. The best part is that your cat won't 'blame' you when it lands on the tape or pan of water. The worktop will lose its feline real estate value.

Double up on these tactics by redirecting your cat to a more acceptable perch, like a sturdy cat tree or wide shelves in your living room that are arranged in a step pattern and feature carpet remnants for your cat to hone her claws as she leaps from one shelf to the next.

Shredding Toilet Paper
SCENARIO:

You enter your bathroom and the full roll of toilet paper litters the floor and sink like white confetti, with your tabby standing proud beside it. Her shredding may also expand to include tissue boxes.

MOTIVATION:

Some cats are highly active and get bored very easily with nothing to do, so they invent their own games while you're gone – like terrorising toilet tissues. In addition, the rolling motion of the toilet paper adds to their glee because they get to scratch and claw at a moving 'prey'.

SOLUTIONS:

The easiest answer is to keep your bathroom door shut, but we are only human after all and the door may be left open by us or by our guests. Instead, instal a toilet roll dispenser, or tuck the roll in a basket with a lid and then place it on an open shelf above the toilet or in the sink cabinet. As for a tissue box, flip it upside down when not in use. If you don't mind cleaning up a little water, place a small cup of water on the toilet paper roll as the noise of the cup hitting the floor and the watery splash may be enough to get your cat to seek other playtime options. This behaviour is a cat's way of telling you that she is bored and needs more fun activities to do during the day.

Some play-motivated cats can be on a roll, literally, by occupying their time by shredding and unravelling your rolls of toilet paper.

Dashing Out the Door
SCENARIO:
Whenever you enter or leave the house, your cat seems to emerge from nowhere and attempts to scurry outside before you can block her path.

MOTIVATION:
What makes an indoor cat feel the need to prowl outside? She smells and hears other cats, especially during the breeding seasons, or she may be just curious. There is also the chance that she spent her kittenhood as an outdoor stray and misses the outdoors.

SOLUTIONS:
Startle the cat with water from a spray bottle, a shake of a can with coins, and say 'back' as you prepare to depart. Or toss her a kitty treat or toy just before you exit to distract. Also, randomly choose different doors to enter and leave. A cat cannot lie in wait at three different exits. It is a good idea to post fluorescent-coloured signs reminding all people in the house to stop and look for signs of the darting feline before opening the door to depart. You can provide her with the great outdoors safely by installing a cat enclosure, but do remember to supervise her when she is in the enclosure.

Invest the time to break your cat of her dangerous habit of trying to bolt out of any door opened to the outside.

Stealing Your Bling
SCENARIO:
Mysteriously, a piece of jewellery is no longer where you last left it. Then you solve this caper after witnessing your cat march off down the hall with said item dangling from her mouth.

MOTIVATION:
Some cats are genuine cat burglars. They can't resist stealing all that glimmers and shines from your dressing table or bathroom shelf. For further proof, simply Google 'feline cat burglars' and up pops a load of YouTube videos catching tabbies in the act. Blame genetics to some extent as certain breeds, including the American Bobtail, Bengal, Munchkin and Pixie Bob, inherit this steal-shiny-stuff behaviour. As indoor hunters, they seek shiny objects to fetch, swat or stash in their kitty lair – usually under your bed or in the corner of a dark wardrobe. Some cats kick into survival mode, stockpiling perceived necessities in secret hiding spots. It's much like the squirrel who stores acorns for the long cold winter.

SOLUTIONS:
It can be pricey to replace jewellery, and your cat's hiding places for their stash of goods may be deep in the sofa cushion or down the kitchen drain. So, protect your bling by getting into the habit of always storing your shiny accessories in a jewellery box – and try not to let your cat see you do it. Redirect your feline thief towards safe, shiny cat toys too. If your cat accelerates this behaviour, she may have an obsessive-compulsive condition and this could signal anxiety issues that need to be addressed by a vet.

Climbing and Clawing
SCENARIO:

Your sofa now bears claw marks scribbled on the armrest and sides. Or you gasp as you witness your feline gymnast scamper up your designer curtains in the living room and then claw her way down, doing her best impression of a firefighter sliding down a fire station pole.

MOTIVATION:

Your cat is not purposely seeking out your most expensive or treasured furnishings. She is behaving much like a feline Zorro, using her claws to declare ownership of her turf. Recognise that cats, just like you, want and desire something they can call their own. With each scratch, sebaceous glands in her paws are released to leave an odour that alerts other feline intruders to back off. She also needs to claw on a sturdy surface to remove the old outer husk of her nails and keep her claws honed. Think of it as a feline pedicure.

SOLUTIONS:

Redirect your cat to a sturdy scratching post sprinkled with catnip. Position this scratching post in a favourite place where your cat spends a lot of time, perhaps in the corner of your living room. Reward your cat with treats and praise when she begins to claw on the scratching post. 'Donate' that old chair, buy a durable scratching post, or give your cat a thick log with bark for sharpening. Place the log vertically because cats like to stretch upwards when they claw.

At the same time, lower the feline real estate value of your sofa and curtains by temporarily applying double-sided tape to the targeted furniture. Cats hate feeling anything sticky on their paw pads. Place long plastic containers filled with an inch of water by the curtains to thwart your cat's jumping desires. You can also spray citronella or another scent cats detest on the fabric – do read the directions beforehand to make sure the spray won't discolour or damage the fabric.

Bullying Your Dog
SCENARIO:
Your tiny tabby boldly sits between your big dog and his food bowl, daring him to approach. Or your cat taunts, stalks and even swats at your sweet dog, causing him to flee in fear.

MOTIVATION:
It is not the size of the cat in a fight, but the size of the fight in the cat. It is all about 'cat-itude' and feline aggression. Your cat's pushy behaviour has so far reaped desired results, a petrified pooch, and they are in control of the house. Without intervention, this bully cat could decide to start pushing you around and making demands for meals on their time schedule and even start nipping your hands.

SOLUTIONS:
Cats sport sharp teeth and sharp claws and are extremely agile, making them a formidable opponent even for dogs 10 times their size. To thwart these cat-on-dog bully episodes, you need to first look for early attack warning signs coming from your cat. These include her dropping her head, raising her back end and shimmying her body. Calmly step in and try distracting your cat by tossing her favourite toy mouse or treat in the opposite direction of your dog. After all, a cat can't be happy and angry at the same time.

You definitely need to keep your pets separated when you are not home to supervise for the safety of your dog. Reintroduce them after both have been exercised and are tired – not at high-excitement times like dinner. Keep your cat's claws trimmed to minimise injuries to your dog.

CHAPTER 6

Basic and Advanced Tricks

Training Tactics

Despite reputations for being aloof, many cats like to ham it up, learn new tricks, and even please us! You need a dash of cat psychology to do so. Unlike happy-to-please dogs, cats need to be convinced that the training is in their best interest.

You need to motivate your cat. Successful cat training is accomplished by employing a pattern of behaviour reinforced by reward. This is called conditioned response, the same principle that bell-ringing Pavlov used to elicit responses from hungry dogs a century ago.

Without even realising it, you've probably been using conditioned response with your cat already. For example, does your cat sprint into the kitchen each time he hears you peel back the tab top on a new tin of cat food, or race there when he hears the whirl of an electric can opener? These sounds serve as cues to your cat that if he ventures into the kitchen, there is a good chance that he will be rewarded with food. Cats are no dummies, and they quickly learn to distinguish the differences in sounds between a can opener and your mobile phone ringtone.

Now here comes the humbling point of cat training: your clever cat is also training you. Conditioned response can be a two-way street. Your cat knows that if he rubs against your leg, there is a strong likelihood that you will acknowledge him and reward this display of affection by petting him or handing him a small treat. In any partnership, success relies on how well the two parties speak the same language.

Before you launch into teaching tricks, devote a few days or the next week to look at your cat in a whole new way. Focus more attention on your cat's actions and habits. By understanding cat chat

This feline appears to be full of suspicion and needs convincing of the rewards he will reap by learning new tricks.

and feline body cues, you will strengthen your communication skills with your cat. For successful training, the trick for you comes in knowing what makes your cat tick. What motivates her?

PRACTISE THE THREE Cs: CLEAR, CONCISE AND CONSISTENT.

Cats are whizzes at reading our body languages, our voice tones, and even our emotions. You achieve a desired behaviour by keeping training sessions free from confusion.

MAKE YOUR TRAINING SESSIONS FUN

Bring plenty of enthusiasm and encouragement to the sessions. If you try to force a trick, become impatient or worse, demanding, your cat is apt to leave the scene. Also, avoid long training sessions because cats can quickly be bored by chores. The cornerstone behind successful training revolves around positive reinforcement. Most cats are willing students when they can work for food rewards. Cats need to know there will be a payoff for their performances.

> ## MINI TRAINING SESSIONS
>
> In all training, it is important to conduct the mini-sessions to gradually build up to the end result. Accept that your cat will let you know when the training session is over by walking away or suddenly have the urge to groom.

The most trainable cats are those with good attention spans, outgoing personalities, and who are highly motivated by food, praise or grooming sessions.

Why Train a Cat?

 Will all this trick training guarantee that your feline friend becomes the next Hollywood cat celebrity? Most likely not. But anything positive you can do to enrich your relationship with your cat is worth the effort. There are several payoffs:

🐾 You build a stronger bond and deeper level of trust with your cat.

🐾 You stimulate your cat's mind and work his muscles.

🐾 You increase his level of self-confidence.

🐾 Schooled cats are less apt to display behavioural problems, often triggered by boredom or the inability to unleash energy.

Cat Training Commandments

If only you could wave a wand and 'poof!', your cat has been transformed into a famous trick performer. Alas, success is all about building on mastering each step. Make training easy and fun for you and your cat by adopting these attitudes and actions:

1 Begin any training session by addressing your cat by his name. This alerts him that you are talking to him, not the dog, not your spouse, and not the ballgame on the TV.

2 Be consistent with your verbal and hand signal cues.

3 Pay attention to your cat's moods. Select training session times when your cat is receptive to learning. Never force training on your cat.

4 Choose a quiet room and time where you can be one-on-one with your cat to teach him a new trick.

5 Bring plenty of enthusiasm and encouragement to the sessions, as well as patience.

6 Deliver food treats and enthusiastic praise immediately after each success, no matter how small. Select your cat's favourite food to motivate him to perform.

7 Begin with the basics: sit, stay, and come.

Use Clickers

Training your cat can be as easy as one, two, click! The clicker is a small, handheld metal device found at pet shops. Depress the metal flap to create the distinctive crisp sound. If you don't have a clicker, you can improvise by making a clicking sound with a ballpoint pen or with your tongue.

Clicker training works a little differently in cats than dogs. With dogs, people want quick performances. With cats, the clicker technique works to shape natural behaviours on command. In time, your cat learns to associate the sound of the clicker with making the right action and earning a treat. In clicker training, timing is paramount. You need to depress the clicker the instant your cat performs each step of the desired behaviour, then treat. Don't wait until he completes a multi-step trick. Once your cat reliably offers the desired behaviour, then only click for the perfect ones or the fast ones. You'll be amazed by the results.

Try Hand Signals Too

One way to reinforce verbal training cues is to pair them with hand signals to convey clear communication to your cat. Teaching a young cat hand signals can be beneficial when he becomes a senior. Hearing diminishes with age, with deafness common among cats 15 years or older. Remember that no cat is ever too old to learn a new signal, so that flicking a light on and off might become the new dinner 'bell', when calling the cat's name no longer works.

THE BEST TIME TO TRAIN

To get your cat into a trick-training mood, first select very alluring treats such as boiled calf liver, chicken or turkey, or pieces of tinned tuna. Time your training sessions before your cat eats a meal, so he is hungry to learn.

---

8 Opt to gradually introduce more advanced commands, such as 'Go find your mouse' or 'Let's go outside for a lead walk'.

9 Tap into your cat's innate curiosity and desire for attention. Let him sniff and examine new toys and training tools.

0 Take a systematic approach to training. Make sure your cat understands each training step before introducing the next. Set your cat up for success, not failure.

1 Stick with mini-training sessions. Cats can quickly be bored by what they perceived to be a chore, so keep training sessions under 5 minutes at a time. Most cats will let you know class is over by walking away or suddenly having an urge to groom.

2 Teach your cat only one new trick at a time. Cats are not multi-tasking masters.

Basic Tricks

With some work and a lot of patience, every cat owner should be able to teach their feline friend how to do basic tricks that will make you feel in control and able to command behaviours with rewards.

COME WHEN CALLED

A popular saying goes, 'Dogs come when they're called. Cats take a message and get back to you later'. It doesn't have to be that way. The 'come' command is a good one to learn if your indoor cat slips out the door to outside or if there is a fire in your house or other emergency that requires you to gather up your cat quickly and exit. A cat who has been conditioned to earn a treat or praise when his owner calls him by name is more apt to come when called.

1 Start by speaking his name in an upbeat, happy tone. When your cat glides into the room and comes into view, offer a friendly greeting and call him by his name. Say, 'Hey Murphy, it's good to see you'.

2 Now, connect his name with the 'come' command by introducing a food signal. Use the sound of the can opener, tap the side of your cat's bowl, or shake a cat treat bag each time you say, 'Murphy, come'. Your cat will quickly learn to associate these sounds and your voice with getting a tasty treat if he enters the room.

3 Call your cat by name and whistle. Tap the food bowl if necessary. You are teaching your cat to associate food with your beckoning whistle.

4 Time your training session. The best time to teach this command is at mealtimes when your cat is highly attentive.

SIT

Cats who sit on cue are more receptive to learning other tricks and behaviours. For this trick, let gravity be your guide.

1 Select a quiet place where your cat feels comfortable and safe. Gently place him on a table near the edge closest to you. Give him some friendly cheek rubs with your finger to put him at ease.

2 Get his attention. Say, 'Murphy, sit' as you move a small, high-quality treat slightly above his eye level and directly over his head.

3 Time when to dole out the treat. When he tips his head back to follow the treat with his eyes, he needs to sit down to maintain his balance. As soon as he sits, say, 'Sit, good sit'. If your cat does not sit when you ask him to, gently press down on his hindquarters. Be gentle and patient so you do not frustrate or frighten your cat.

4 Repeat these steps in 5-minute training sessions until your cat obeys the 'sit' cue with only a hand gesture and not a treat.

5 Once your cat sits on command from a tabletop, you can practise this command when he is on the floor.

Wow your friends by showing how smart – and obedient – your cat is when he heeds your 'sit' cue.

 TAKE TWO: Now that your cat is sitting on cue, it's time for the next challenge of teaching him to sit up. Time the training when your cat is calm and happy. With your cat sitting on a sturdy chair or on the floor, hold a treat an inch or so over his head and say, 'Sit up'. If he tries to swat at the treat with his paw or stands up on his hind legs and grabs your hand, don't surrender the treat to him. Look for the weight shift. Repeat the cue, 'Sit up' while holding the treat over his head. When he sits up and balances his weight over his hind feet, reward him with the treat and praise him. Repeat the cue-behaviour-reward sequence several times in a 5-minute training session to reinforce the behaviour.

STAY

Face the facts, you will never outsprint your feline. Nor can you match his ability to zigzag or dart under the bed, especially when you bring out the car carrier to take him to the dreaded veterinary clinic. Save yourself some time and frustration by teaching your cat to stay on cue.

1. Start the training in an enclosed room like a screened porch or small bedroom. You want a place where your cat cannot escape or hide. (Close the closet doors before you begin.) If your cat starts to move away from you, say his name followed by 'Stay'.

2. Then extend one arm straight out and with the palm facing down. Move your palm down steadily towards the floor. Do not chase after your cat. Maintain your standing position and remain calm. Only after he sits should you approach him slowly, kneel down, and reward him with a treat and praise.

3. Pick up and cuddle your cat. Then put him back on the ground. Watch his movements and immediately reward him each time he stays in place.

4. Repeat until he stays in position readily after hearing the 'stay' cue.

TAKE TWO: Once your cat obeys the 'stay' in the enclosed room, practise this trick in a large, spacious room like the living room or kitchen. By teaching your cat to stay, your cat-chasing days are thankfully over.

Cats who master the art of fetching clearly demonstrate their hunting skills and recognition of you as someone they wish to impress.

FETCH

Cats are born predators who love to chase, stalk and capture. Shape those instinctive drives into teaching your cat how to fetch. A key to success is to select a large open space or long hallway free of obstacles or distractions.

1 Take a piece of paper and mash it into a wad as your cat watches and hears that tempting crinkling sound. Show your cat the paper wad and then toss it over his head as you say, 'Fetch'.

2 Put a lot of positive praise in your voice as your cat scurries after the paper wad, bats it around, and pounces on it. Use your hand to motion your cat to come back to you as you say, 'Come here'.

3 You may need to show him at first by retrieving the paper wad a few times until he understands how to play this game. Then give him a treat each time he brings back the paper wad, even if he is within a foot of you.

 TAKE TWO: Invite a friend to play fetch with you and your cat. Position you and your friend on opposite ends of the hallway or room and your cat in the middle. Toss the paper wad just over your cat's head towards your friend. Praise him when he gives chase. Then have your friend toss the paper way over your cat's head in your direction. Again, praise and treat.

YOU CAN TOUCH THIS

Cats who like to shake paws are natural candidates to learn how to touch an object on cue.

1 Place your cat on a sturdy table and give him the 'sit' cue. Position him about 12 in (6 cm) from the edge of the table.

2 Place a small toy, a thick book, or an object that won't tip over when touched at the edge of the table between you and your cat.

3 Hold a small treat in front of your cat, making sure that the object is between the treat and your cat.

4 Give your cat the 'paw' cue paired with his name (example: 'Murphy, paw') as you touch the object with the hand not holding the treat.

5 As soon as your cat reaches for the treat with one of his front paws and touches or steps on the object, hit the clicker or say, 'Paw, good paw.' Immediately give him the treat and praise him.

6 If your cat isn't touching the object, try moving it side to side to entice him into trying to swat it. As soon as he touches the object, press the clicker and/or say, 'Paw, good paw', and hand over the treat so he begins to associate the object with getting a food reward.

7 Repeat the above steps in a 5-minute training session. Your cat may touch the object with his left or right paw or alternate.

GIMME FIVE

Dogs don't have a monopoly when it comes to greeting houseguests by shaking paws or touching objects. You can train your social cat to be a feline greeter who lightly raises his paw and touches the palm of your guests.

1 Start with a handful of treats that your cat craves. Sit on the floor with your cat, holding the treats in one hand.

2 Ask your cat to 'sit' (or use a treat over his head to get him to sit).

3 Hold your treat hand just slightly in front of your cat's eyes and wait. When he lifts a front paw off the floor, immediately say, 'Shake' and give him a treat.

4 Repeat this until your cat raises his paw whenever your hand is at eye level. Say 'Shake, good shake', and treat each time.

5 Once your cat puts his paw up whenever your hand is raised to his eye level, say, 'High five' and click and treat.

6 Repeat these steps four or five times per session. Stop once your cat delivers a couple of paw shakes or gets bored.

FAMOUS FELINE TRICKSTERS

Certainly any cat can become a master at learning tricks, even mixed breeds. Need proof? The famous Morris the Cat (and many orange tabbies taking on this role as a pitch cat for a commercial cat food brand) was a former shelter cat adopted by a professional animal trainer named Rose Ordile.

Ordile relied on positive reinforcement and conditional response techniques to train Morris and other celebrity animals. She started feeding Morris in a studio chair, keeping his bowl there at mealtimes. She taught him to stay in this chair and that made him camera ready for his close-ups during tapings.

Some cat breeds seem to be born with the performing gene more than others. They tend to be athletic, outgoing breeds, such as the Siamese, Abyssinian and Maine Coon.

Advanced Training

If you have a highly motivated cat who enjoys performing in front of an audience, he may be ideally suited for learning more complicated tricks. The training sessions can also strengthen the bond between you both.

WALK ON A LEAD

Confident, curious cats that are begging to explore outdoors can do so safely when tethered to you with a lead. In order to teach your cat to walk on a lead, you must first recognise that cats won't walk long distances or heel obediently by your side like dogs do.

Cats prefer to take in their surroundings. Expect your cat to take a few steps, stop and sniff or perk his ears into the wind or cackle at birds out of reach. The outdoor walk should be timed during a quiet time and be conducted in a safe, dog-free place such as a fenced backyard or other location to make this a pleasant experience for your cat.

1 Select a cat harness from a pet shop that fits the barrel of your cat's torso and a lightweight cat lead.

2 Introduce these two items by placing them near your cat's scratching post or favourite napping spot for a week to let him investigate them on his own terms.

3 Fit your cat in the harness without the lead for a minute or so and let him walk around the house. Make this a positive experience by heaping on the food treats and praise. Gradually increase the time your cat wears the harness indoors.

4 Add the lead to the harness and again, let your cat walk around indoors. Remember to praise and give treats.

5 Hook the lead to the harnessed cat and lead your cat around the house by holding a small food treat in front of your cat's nose. Once your cat appears comfortable and confident walking indoors, cradle him (attached to the lead) in your arms and walk around outside. Speak calmly and point out cool sights for a few minutes before heading back indoors and giving him a treat.

6 Once your cat has mastered all these steps, go outside with him and gently lower him to the ground. Kneel down beside him and speak calmly as he starts to explore with you holding the lead. Spend a few minutes outdoors before going back inside and treating him.

TEACHING YOUR CAT TO TRAVEL BY PUSHCHAIR

A safe option to exposing your confident and curious indoor cat to the outdoors is to give him a ride in a pushchair. This is a rare mode of transport but you may find that it suits your cat's needs.

1 Select a pet pushchair or stroller that will accommodate your cat's size. Tap into his curious nature by allowing him to investigate it on his own terms inside your home for a few days.

2 Make the pushchair more appealing by placing treats on the wheels and in the seat for him to sniff and find.

3 Place your cat in the pushchair and give him a treat or a small meal.

4 Casually close the lid with your cat inside for a few seconds and then lift the lid. Repeat and treat when your cat stays inside the pushchair.

5 Put on your cat's harness and lead and place him in the pushchair in your home. Make a short, slow test drive down your hallway to get him used to the motion of the stroller. Praise him and give him a small treat when he is sitting still.

6 If he jumps out of the pushchair, gently place him back in and praise and treat him when he sits down. Timing is important: you want to reinforce the desired behaviour with a reward.

7 Expand the pushchair time to your drive and gradually down your pavement on a pleasant day. Walk slowly but steadily.

Expand your cat's world by getting him accustomed to riding in style in a pushchair designed for felines.

CHAPTER 7
Indoor Life

The Great Indoors

Take a moment and look at life from your feline's point of view. She truly makes an ideal house-mate, but even cats have a limit to their patience and tolerance and need to be stimulated when in the home.

When you come home after a bad day, you can usually count on your cat to greet you with soft eyes and a steady, soothing purr. Without saying a human word, she calms you, reduces your blood pressure and makes you feel like you're worth a million bucks. Count your blessings you live with a cat because they tolerate a whole lot more than most two-leggers would, especially indoor cats who are around that much more.

Indoor cats tend to live longer and safer lives than outdoor cats, but all those hours spent inside without the proper feline-enriching amenities can test their patience and tax your sanity. A bored kitty may act out by boycotting the litter box, scaling the curtains or shredding the sofa. There is a solution in the form of a home makeover. Don't worry, these feline-fine furnishings and do-it-yourself strategy suggestions won't make your home look catty or strain your budget. To get into the feline cat decor mindset, first think like a cat. As a species noted for being both prey and predator, cats need to feel safe and they need to hunt – even if the targeted 'prey' is a toy mouse, wand toy, or a songbird on the tree branch near the living room window.

The latest trend in home decorating centres on how to strike the balance of meeting the needs of indoor cats while still making interiors look attractive.

Cat Decor

Cats have natural needs: to hunt; to catch, to kill; to eat; to groom; to play; and to sleep. Whether you own or rent, prefer to purchase or are into DIY projects, improve your interior for your indoor cat.

RESIST BEING A SQUARE THINKER.

The amount of floor space you have isn't as important as how you utilise floor-to-ceiling space for your indoor cats. Think in terms of vertical space and cubic space instead of focusing on your available square metraage.

CONSIDER FLOOR-TO-CEILING POSTS.

Bring out the mountain lion in your cat! If you have floor-to-ceiling posts, wrap them in thick sisal rope. Or, buy floor-to-ceiling posts that you can remove when you move. Many cats like to sharpen their claws and show off their climbing skills. Sisal rope is available at DIY centres.

INVEST IN LITTER BOX HIDEAWAYS.

Achieve a win-win for you and your feline by furnishing discreet litter hideaways inside decorative end tables or other pieces of furniture known as 'catinets' and 'catcubes'. Scoop daily and clean the litter boxes weekly with mild soap to keep your home smelling fresh.

HAVE A 21ST CENTURY CAT SCRATCHING POST.

Your modern-day cat deserves modern-day furniture. Replace that wobbly, carpet-lined, inverted T-shaped scratching post with modular structures that can be quickly and easily reconfigured and expanded into a feline playground with various levels, hideaways, dangling toys and ramps – all in eye-catching designs. Go beyond carpeted scratching posts to ones featuring surfaces with sisal, jute and corrugated cardboard.

SCRATCHING POSTS

Cats scratch up and down, side to side, and at angles. Bypass those cheap scratching posts at the pet or pound shop and choose a scratching post that offers these three angles for scratching. Pick posts that are steady and sturdy because if they are lightweight and wobble, your cat will dismiss them and make a beeline to your sofa or recliner when she gets the itch to scratch.

Fortunately, there are many different designs so you can select one that blends into your decor and wins over your cat. Do not get a used cat scratching post or tree. Cats often don't like to share with strangers and may give this furniture a sniff or two and ignore it.

OFFER A LOFTY PERCH.

Cats like surveying their surroundings and viewing the outside world from a high, safe place. So, provide a sturdy, machine-washable window perch or two and, perhaps, position a tall cat tree near your sliding glass door to give your cat the chance to see eye-to-eye with a bird in flight. Or hoist a cat trapeze that enhances your cat's fitness and offers a comfy off-the-ground napping spot. These options allow her to be perched up high – and out of reach of a crying toddler or the family's overly playful Beagle.

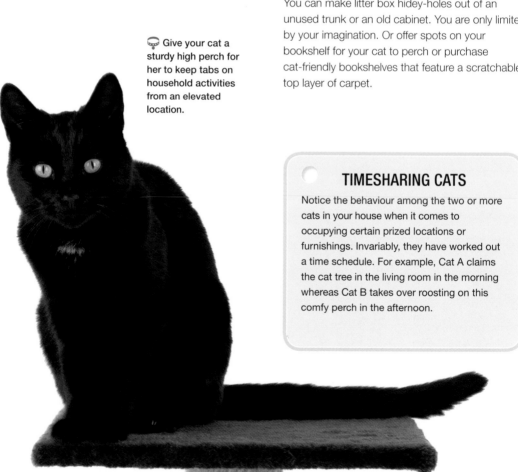

💬 Give your cat a sturdy high perch for her to keep tabs on household activities from an elevated location.

CREATE A FELINE WALL HIGHWAY.

Instead of hanging pictures on your living room wall, install sturdy and eye-catching catwalk shelves. Ideally, catwalks should be about 60 cm (2 ft) wide so that two approaching cats can easily pass one another. Provide various ways for cats to access these catwalks such as ramps, mini-stairs, or from the top of the sofa. If you rent, you can easily patch and paint the walls without losing your security deposit when you move out.

BE CREATIVE.

You can make litter box hidey-holes out of an unused trunk or an old cabinet. You are only limited by your imagination. Or offer spots on your bookshelf for your cat to perch or purchase cat-friendly bookshelves that feature a scratchable top layer of carpet.

TIMESHARING CATS

Notice the behaviour among the two or more cats in your house when it comes to occupying certain prized locations or furnishings. Invariably, they have worked out a time schedule. For example, Cat A claims the cat tree in the living room in the morning whereas Cat B takes over roosting on this comfy perch in the afternoon.

SCHEDULE DAILY PLAYTIME.

Set aside 5 to 10 minutes each morning and night for play sessions with your cat. Drag a feather wand across the floor or toss paper wads or catnip-filled toys for your cat to leap and try to catch. By interacting with your cat at night, you stand a better chance for a good night's sleep because they will be tired and ready to snooze too.

TOYS WITH EXPIRATION DATES

Catnip (known as *Nepeta cataria* for those botanical buffs) is a proud member of the mint family and the oil from catnip leaves contains a chemical called nepetalactone. One good whiff and your cat is apt to fling the catnip-filled toy high in the air, pounce on it and roll on it for 5 to 15 minutes. You may think your cat is acting like a fool, but the catnip toy is providing purposeful play and exercise so your indoor cat doesn't get mistaken for a hairy piece of furniture. To maximise its potency, select toys filled with certified-organic catnip and toys with openings that allow you to regularly replace the stale herb with fresh, aromatic catnip.

Store the unused catnip in an airtight bag out of direct sunlight. For the price of a latte, you can treat your cat to a week's worth of bliss-filled fun.

Take the time to marvel at how athletic, agile and quick your cat is during interactive play sessions.

'In' Cat Hidden Dangers

Your pink-nosed cat napping on a windowsill may never step a paw outside, but she is still at risk for surprising health dangers such as severe sunburns and solar-induced cancer if not properly protected. Topping the list of being most vulnerable to the sun's damageing rays while lounging indoors are any cats with light-coloured coats, pink or pale-coloured noses, little to no hair on their underbellies or those whose coats have been shaved. Dark-nosed pets with brown or black coats are at less risk from developing skin cancer.

Solar-induced cancers, such as squamous cell carcinoma, are often located on the belly, inner lips, noses, lips, eyelids and ears of pets. Other sun-causing skin cancers include basal cell carcinoma and melanoma. How does this happen? Well, solar damage results from absorption of ultraviolet light into skin molecules. Fortunately, early detection of skin cancers increases chances of cures when treated promptly. To protect your indoor cat from being exposed to harmful UVA and UVB rays, take these precautionary measures:

DODGE THE SUN'S STRONGEST RAYS.

Protect your indoor cats who love napping on sunny window ledges by installing window treatments that filter ultraviolet rays without restricting sunlight. Tint your windows or instal solar control roller blinds or honeycomb blinds.

THINK NORTH AND SOUTH.

Only allow your cat access to window perches placed in windows facing north and south to avoid the harshest sun rays in the morning (east windows) and the afternoon (west windows).

Keep your sun-seeking indoor cat safe by installing window perches out of direct sunlight.

CAT-SAFE OUTDOOR AREA

Treat your indoor cat to safe outdoor access. Instead of harnessing her and trying to time your walk when none of the neighborhood dogs are also on the sidewalk, consider adding a 'catio' – an enclosed patio designed especially for cats. A catio provides a fully protected outdoor environment for otherwise indoor cats. The perks are access to fresh air, the chance to bask in sunlight, and protection from predators. There are various styles of catios. Depending on your space and your budget, you can accessorise your feline's catio with cat perches, a litter box, corrugated scratching products and even a fun cat tunnel.

If you love to garden and allow your supervised cat to have access to your backyard, then choose your flowers with your cat's safety in mind. To protect your cat from being stung by busy bees on pollinating missions, select flowers that attract butterflies more than bees. Topping the list are red roses, zinnias and jasmine.

Most cats can't resist wanting to swat at flying insects or bees, so take precautions to keep your cat safe when outdoors.

CHAPTER 8
Litter Training

Litter Boxes

One of the most crucial must-have items in any cat household is the right litter box. Picking the perfect one can mean the difference in your cat using it – or boycotting it.

From the start, set out the right litter box environment for your feline. Cats prefer litter boxes in quiet places inside the home that provide them with privacy. They also need places that provide them with escape routes. Cats need to see what's coming at them while inside a litter box and feel protected. Bad locations are inside the shower stall, down in a damp, dark basement, next to a furnace or water heater, or in a high-traffic area like next to the back door. A common reason for a cat to bypass the litter box is because it is located in hard-to-squeeze-in locations or, worse, in high-traffic areas like the back door leading into the kitchen, or in noisy areas like next to a basement furnace or the washer and dryer. These places may be convenient or out of sight for you, but your cat might find them too noisy or scary.

Use the formula of one litter box per cat plus one. For example, if you have two cats, you need three litter boxes. Giving your cats choices increases the likelihood that they will routinely use the litter box instead of your carpet. Locate a litter box on each level of your home, even if you have only one cat.

Selecting the Right Litter Box

Who knew that there would be so many choices when it comes to selecting a 'toilet' for your cat? These days, litter boxes come in many shapes and sizes. Some even are hidden in decorative end tables in living rooms.

SIZE MATTERS.

An average size litter box may offer ample space for a small Siamese, but be a tight squeeze for a big-boned Maine Coon. Giant cats, like a 7 kg (16 lb) orange tabby, may be better suited for a large plastic box used to store clothing under a bed. These plastic boxes are inexpensive and available at major hardware shops. Conversely, young kittens are better suited for small litter boxes with low sides for easy access. If you have a large adult cat and a small kitten, you can always use the big plastic box for the large cat and the matching lid for the kitten. The lid can also accommodate special needs cats like an old cat who has trouble climbing in and out of the litter box.

TO COVER OR NOT TO COVER.

The answer depends on your cat. Some cats like entering a cave-like structure to eliminate, but others do not. A lid can trap odours and prevent the cat from monitoring its surroundings, placing it in a vulnerable position from another cat or dog. Go without a cover at first and see how your cat reacts. If you go with a lid, you need to be diligent in cleaning out the box daily.

TYPES OF LITTER.

Again, the answer will come from your cat as to whether clumping, clay, pellet or other type of litter material is the preferred choice. Most cats tend to like fine-grain litters that feel soft under their paws, like clumping litter. The reason some cats go on carpets or on a clean pile of clothes is that they seek a substrate that gives them a softer feel than what is inside their litter boxes. Some of the large-sized crystallised pellets are not designed with a cat's needs in mind. A cat thinks 'no way' when he steps on this pea-sized gravel.

THE DEAL ON DEPTH.

Get out your ruler and measure the litter to a depth of 40–50 mm (1½ in to 2 in) and you will meet the needs of most cats. But cats who like slick smooth surfaces will fare better with just a thin layer of litter. So, please don't empty a 2.25 kg (5 lb) bag of litter into a box and think that you now won't have to worry about cleaning it out every day. That depth could be too deep and the smell may cause your cat to seek other places in the house to eliminate.

Experiment by offering your newly adopted cat or kitten a pair of litter boxes filled with two different types of litter to discover her preference.

Routine Clean

Offering litter box cleaning guidance to people has proven to go a long way in keeping cats in homes – and preventing guests from sniffing out unpleasant pet odours when they come through the front door.

Picture for a moment your home minus a clean bathroom, and your only option being that of a pungent port-a-potty in the backyard. You would find yourself wishing for the lung capacity of an Olympic swimmer so that you can hold your breath and complete your deed before you need to inhale. Disgusting, right? Some cats belonging to delinquent litter-box-scooping owners feel the same way. An important reality check is that litter boxes do not magically clean themselves – and that includes even those so-called 'automatic' litter boxes. Sooner or later, you will need to scoop, bag and discard your cat's pungent deposits.

One source of pride among cat owners conscious about cleaning litter boxes daily is when guests are surprised that the home contains a cat or two because no litter box odour can be detected.

PRACTISE SCOOP PATROL, DAILY.

Scooping out the urine and faeces from the litter box each day is not one of life's favourite pastimes. Remind yourself that this diligence pays dividends because your actions encourage your cat to use his litter box and not seek other places in your home to make unwanted 'deposits'.

PRACTISE COMMON SENSE ON SCENTS.

If you keep the litter box scooped daily and cleaned weekly, you won't have to worry about visitors casting their noses in the air and declaring, 'Oh, you have a cat'. Remember, the feline sense of smell is far keener than ours. Cats are strongly influenced by odours. I advise against using scented litters or room deodorisers placed next to or, worse, inside the litter box. These smells are too pungent for most cats and may prompt your cat to seek an alternative toilet in your home – such as the living room carpet.

CLEAN-UP TIPS

Cats are fastidious by nature so a dirty litter box is horrid. They deserve having you scoop out the urine and faeces from their litter boxes daily. Keeping litter boxes clean may prevent your cat from being tempted to eliminate in other places of the house.

⦅⦆ Remove the litter entirely and clean the boxes with mild dishwashing soap and warm water every week. If possible, allow the litter boxes to air-dry in the sun to kill germs. If you do use bleach to disinfect the boxes, use a very weak solution and rinse thoroughly before drying. The strong odour of bleach can be a turnoff to your cat. I recommend that you have a spare litter box filled with fresh litter while the other boxes are drying. Or, clean one litter box at a time so that your cat can always find an appropriate spot to go.

⦅⦆ Skip scented litter and never plug in an air freshener in an outlet next to the litter box to mask the odour. Cats hate perfumed scents and may opt to boycott the box altogether.

Clearing the Air

The pungent smell of feline urine, faeces or vomit can stubbornly lodge inside the fibres of your carpet and even your hardwood floor. Avoid using household cleaners containing ammonia because, unfortunately, ammonia is a by-product of urine and will actually beckon your cat back to the spot. Likewise, vinegar temporarily snuffs out the odour but is not powerful enough to completely erase the smell that will return. If you consider commercial steam-cleaning services, often the cleaning crew does a great job ridding your carpeting of ordinary dirt but the heat from the steam machine actually bakes the organic stains into your carpet fibres. A day or more after they leave, the feline-causing foul smell is likely to come back. Finally, vigorous rubbing with cleaning wipes on a stain site only drives the urine deeper into your carpet and pad. Instead, oust these odours and stymie those stains by following these steps:

1 Be quick and address the stain before it gets a chance to seep into the carpet or hardwood or dry.

2 Soak up as much of the foul liquid as you can with kitchen towels or old cotton towels or rags. Blot towels on the surface until you no longer see any telltale yellow moisture.

3 Neutralise the odour with a chemical ally. Keep in mind that your feline's smelly 'deposits' consist of protein chemicals so the best weapon to defeat the odour is to attack it with commercial pet-stain products containing protein enzymatic solutions. Follow and heed the label directions closely and be patient. Some of the most effective enzymatic cleaners may need a day to render the stain odour free.

4 If your cat's target is your bedspread or other machine-washable item, add bicarbonate of soda into your washing machine along with your detergent and wash the soiled item in cold water. Bicarbonate of soda has a long reputation for effectively absorbing odours. Don't use hot water because it can seal the odour into fabric.

SNIFFING OUT ODOURS

Your nose confirms your cat did use someplace in your home as a toilet, but you can't find the location. Don't panic. You need to shed some light on this dilemma. Buy a black light bulb at a hardware shop and screw it into a portable lamp. At night, turn off your lights in the suspected room and sweep the area with this lit lamp. Old pet stains emit a greenish fluorescent glow. Place a kitchen towel on the site, turn on the lights and you're ready to get rid of this odour-generating hidden stain.

If your cat is turning his nose up at using a dirty litter box, you can bet the odour is detectable in your house.

Potty Training

If you are adopting an adult cat or a kitten – or relocating to a new home with your resident cat – the most important lesson to teach them is to find and use the litter box.

Feline bathroom behaviour is no laughing matter for people and is literally life-or-death for far too many cats. The number one behavioural reason cats are booted out of homes and discarded at animal shelters is because of inappropriate elimination. Certainly, no one likes to come home and be bombarded by the stench of cat urine or discover a poop pile on the living room rug. Some people understandably become tired of cleaning up messes on their carpets, floors and even their beds. Or one spouse will deliver an ultimatum: either persuade the cat to use the litter box or get rid of the cat.

There are many legitimate reasons that some cats bypass the litter box and go elsewhere. The true cause may be a medical condition or stress-induced changes in the home routine or a dislike of the available 'facilities'. Either way, your cat is conveying that something is wrong. It is up to us to act like pet detectives and track down clues.

Tutoring Kittens

How you train your young kitten to use the litter box will go a long way in ensuring he practises a lifetime of good bathroom habits. Cats instinctively bury their faeces and cover up urine deposits, a behaviour that dates back thousands of years to when wild cats needed to avoid detection by possible predators. That's why outdoor cats choose the garden or sandbox for toileting, much to the dismay of gardeners and parents.

Most kittens learn the litter box basics from their mothers by about 4 weeks of age. However, kittens who are orphaned or weaned away from their mothers at a very early age may be clueless about litter box etiquette. Set your kitty student up for toileting success by heeding these four tips:

Kittens are curious about everything, including the litter box. Make it more accessible by selecting low-level litter box designs.

1 Select a small litter box with low sides (no higher than 75 mm/3 in) so your short-legged kitten can easily climb in and out.

2 Show and place your new kitten in his litter box. Gently move his front paws through the litter to let him feel the texture. Then let him explore the litter box and jump out on his own. During the next few days, place him in the litter box when he first wakes up, after he eats, after a play session, and after he wakes from a catnap.

3 Scoop out the deposits daily to keep the litter box clean.

4 Finally practise the Two P's of Potty Training: Patience and Punishment-Free. It may take your youngster just a few trips to the litter box to get the hang of things or it may take a few weeks. Resist the temptation to scold or yell or squirt him with a water bottle, because the punishment approach usually backfires. Your kitten may become so frightened that he starts to avoid the litter box and hunts for less scary places like under your bed or in your wardrobe.

Try Faux Pheromones

Before you rush with a guilty verdict in assuming your cat is willfully boycotting the litter box, put on your 'pet detective' trench coat and study the clues. If the cause of your cat boycotting the litter box is indeed behavioural – perhaps in response to a change in the household scene (like a new pet or the departure of a beloved person heading to uni), there is help to restore the pleasant smell back in your home.

But first a little kitty chemistry lesson is warranted. Urine-marking cats leave messages about their mood and their health in the pheromones released in these urine episodes. There is a product called Feliway that has been demonstrated to be effective in curbing behaviour-related urine marking. Feliway is a chemical version of the feline facial pheromone. It works because cats tend not to urine-mark locations where they have already left their facial pheromones. This product comes in a spray as well as a diffuser that plugs into an electric outlet. The diffuser emits this synthetic scent (you can't smell it) 24 hours a day and lasts for about a month. You can spray Feliway directly onto urine marks and household items such as sofas, curtains and door frames without worrying that it will cause a stain.

In extreme cases, urine-marking cats may need calming medications for a period of time. Studies have shown that these drugs can reduce incidents of urine marking up to 75 per cent. Work closely with your vet in administering these medications and then gradually wean your cat off them.

Boycotting the Litter Box

SITUATION:

Your cat may have faithfully used the litter box since day 1 of arriving into your home, but now you find him urinating and defecating outside the box. You can't figure out why this deviation in his toileting habits.

SOLUTION:

Be attentive to your cat's litter box habits. Very often, the reason a cat stops using a litter box is because of a medical or physical condition. A urinary tract or bladder infection, an injury, intestinal parasites – there are many causes. Inappropriate or difficult and frequent urination, appetite loss, listlessness, blood in the urine or frequent licking of the genitals may indicate feline lower urinary tract disease (FLUTD). This is painful inflammation of the lower urinary tract that has the potential to be fatal quickly.

If a cat experiences pain while urinating or eliminating, he may associate the litter box itself with the pain and go elsewhere in an attempt to find a more comfortable spot. Whenever a cat displays a change in elimination habits, book an appointment with your vet, who will perform a thorough physical exam to rule out any medical or life-threatening problems.

In a multi-cat household, locate litter boxes in different rooms to reduce the risk of one cat bullying the other in attempts to use the toilet.

Defecating Outside the Litter Box

SITUATION:

You may find yourself perplexed by your cat who dutifully urinates in his litter box but chooses to defecate elsewhere, such as in the bath or even on the tile floor next to the litter box.

SOLUTION:

The one saving grace is that your cat is targeting easy-to-clean flooring surfaces rather than carpets or furniture. Having become accustomed to using the smooth surface, he is continuing to find a familiar surface. Your cat may be trying to tell you that he is not liking the litter box shape or size, the location, or the type of litter. If this is the case, add a second litter box of a different size without a hood. Position this one near the 'scene of his poo crimes' but do not put in any litter. Instead, leave it empty or place a liner inside to create a smooth surface to attract your cat. You may discover that he appreciates this new feline toilet, customised to his liking.

When your cat suddenly stops using the litter box, book a veterinary appointment. He may have developed a lower urinary tract disease.

Surprise Attacks

SITUATION:

You share your home with two cats who adore you. However, the more outgoing feline seems to delight in making surprise attacks on the more reserved kitty when he is using the litter box. Now, he is opting to go elsewhere.

SOLUTION:

In a multi-cat situation, it is far too common for a dominant cat to bully or pick on a shy cat. The first thing you need to do is add two more litter boxes in different rooms. The bully cat cannot guard three litter boxes at one time. With more spots to choose from, he may feel less inclined to protect 'his' litter box. Position the new litter boxes away from walls and in more open areas so your shy cat can view the room or see if your attack cat is approaching.

Tempting as it is, do not yell at the dominant cat. You will only escalate the tension and anxiety that both animals are feeling. Instead, distract this cat when you see your shy cat head to a litter box by engageing him in play or bribing him with a treat.

CHAPTER 9

Travel

Travelling with Your Cat

Most cats are homebodies, who prefer catnapping on your bed to being unceremoniously glided into a pet carrier that is then strapped to a seat belt inside a vehicle for destinations unknown. The thing you need to do is learn the best way to travel with your cat.

Most cats practise what I call feline algebra: C (Car) + C (Carrier) = C (Veterinary Clinic). That is an equation that can cause much disdain and even a bit of fright in some felines. But there are exceptions. There are cats who crave exploring new places. Count your blessings if you have such a travel kitty. Your four-legged travel mate can make the miles less boring or monotonous.

On the Road

 Before your next road trip, save time on your packing process by heeding these travel tips:

TRAVEL BY CARRIER.

Keep your cat in a pet carrier connected to a seat belt when travelling in your vehicle. Never let your cat roam freely in the vehicle because she can escape when the door opens or try to get under the accelerator.

BANISH FRONT SEAT RIDERS.

Don't be distracted by having your cat ride on the front passenger seat. Keep her safe by having her in a pet carrier tethered to a seat belt in the middle seat. In a collision powerful enough to activate the air bags in the front seats, the force of the air bag inflating can crush or possibly kill your cat.

HARNESS UP.

Play it safe, for your cat's sake, by keeping her fitted in a harness inside the pet carrier. Once arriving at your destination, keep the car doors closed and latch the leash to the harness. To prevent a feline Houdini act, don't let your cat out of the carrier. A fleeing cat won't suddenly stop and race back when you call her name like some dogs will.

BEAT THE HEAT.

During the drive, attach a crate fan to help keep your pet cool. Freeze a couple plastic containers or bottles of water and position them so your cat can curl up around – instant air conditioning! Senior pets and cats with flat faces or short noses (such as Persians) can quickly succumb to heat extremes.

WHAT TO PACK
DISPOSABLE LITTER BOXES.

Lightweight, recyclable plastic boxes with peel-off lids that contain fresh litter are great, if you can get hold of them. There are also easy-to-clean foldable litter boxes made of canvas. Don't forget a litter scoop and spare disposable potty bags.

PORTABLE WATER AND FOOD BOWLS.
Save packing space by using collapsible bowls.

AMPLE SUPPLY OF YOUR CAT'S FOOD (TINNED AND/OR DRY).
Do not switch diets on the road as cats sport sensitive digestive systems and the trip has probably added to the stress level.

FAVOURITE CAT BED AND TOY.
Again, aim for a bed that folds up and does not take up a lot of space.

SPARE LEASH AND COLLAR WITH ID TAG.
Play it safe by packing an extra leash and collar containing the name of your pet and your mobile phone number.

CLEAN-UP PRODUCTS.
Address feline toilet 'oopsies' with a protein enzymatic commercial cleaner, paper towels, and anti-bacterial soap.

PLAY IT SAFE.
Pack a pet first-aid kit in your luggage and enroll in a vet-approved pet first-aid class before your trip.

Move over, dogs. Some cats enjoy travelling with their favourite people to new places just as much as some canines do.

HOTEL FEES

Select hotels that don't take a big bite out of your wallet. Before booking a reservation, make sure you are aware of all hotel fees, including ones for your pet. Some hotels may charge a fee for cleaning up after your pet has stayed. See if you belong to any organisation that offers hotel discounts.

Finding a Pet-Welcoming Hotel

 If you decide to take your cat along on holiday a bit of research about places to stay is necessary. These tips will help to guarantee that the hotel staff will put out the welcome mat for your four-legged travel mate:

HIT THE INTERNET BEFORE YOU HIT THE ROAD.

With the popularity of pets joining their people on road trips, there are more pet travel websites that offer details on pet-welcoming hotels and specific pet policies. Seek pet websites that include candid guest reviews of stays at various hotels.

HEED THE HOTEL RULES.

Some hotels prohibit leaving pets in your hotel room unsupervised. Other guests do not want to hear howling cats who may be frightened and wondering where you are when you want to go out for dinner or sightsee. Budget to include paying for a visit by a professional pet sitter for times you will be out and about without your cat.

PACK PET AMENITIES.

To help your cat feel more at home inside the hotel room, be sure to bring familiar items bearing her scent, such as her bed or her favourite toy.

DISH UP BOTTLED WATER.

Travel can cause gastrointestinal upset in some pets, so stick with bottled water and her brand of pet food during your hotel stays.

LET'S SEE SOME ID.

Always carry a copy of your cat's health records with you, including ID cards with their photos. Make sure your cat has been microchipped and that her collar tag lists your mobile phone number. Some hotels also add temporary tags bearing their phone number during your stay.

SNIFF OUT NEARBY PET PLACES.

Before booking a hotel, find out the contact information on the nearest emergency veterinary clinic, including directions from the hotel. Also consult the hotel's concierge staff about available professional pet sitters.

SPEAK UP FOR SPECIAL ROOMS.

Request a wheelchair-accessible room if available, because the bathrooms are larger and more spacious – providing ample space for your travelling cats to roost safely without escaping.

CAT-PROOFING YOUR HOTEL ROOM

Cats are quite adept at reading our moods. That's why it is important to convey calmness and confidence during any travels. Once inside your room and before you let your cat out of the carrier, do a thorough safety check. Follow this checklist:

- Shut the wardrobe door.
- Put down the toilet lid.
- Block the space under the bed with luggage or other items to prevent your cat from crawling under and hiding in the middle under a king-sized bed out of your reach.
- Position the litter box under the bathroom sink and the travel bowls containing food and bottled water in an opposite corner of the bathroom.
- Place a large towel or blanket on top of the bedspread if your pet sleeps on a bed.
- Hang a 'Do Not Disturb' sign on your door to prevent unexpected visits by hotel staff.

During your stay, try to make friends with the hotel staff. Alert them that you have a cat in the room and be sure to tip generously to encourage the hotel to maintain its pet-welcoming policy. Also set a good example for the next person travelling with his or her pet. Abide by the pet rules and always leave a generous tip for the housekeeping staff. These gestures create a positive impression that will benefit other pet lovers.

Travelling by Plane

If you are fortunate enough to have a cat who loves to travel or you need to transport your cat across country or to a different country, heed these tips to ensure a safe and peaceful flight:

1 Before booking your ticket, check with the airport and government about any legal and stipulated requirements or paperwork and whether your cat needs to travel in the hold.

2 Time your cat's travel health appointment with your vet. Most airlines require proof from your vet that your feline is healthy.

3 Limit your cat's food intake the morning of your flight, especially if she is prone to motion sickness.

4 Harness and leash your cat before you reach airport security. You must remove your cat out of her carrier at the screening, so having her in a harness and leash lessens her chance of scooting out of your arms and escaping in the airport.

5 Keep your cat in the carrier during the flight. Respect your fellow passengers who may have pet allergies or be afraid of pets.

6 Stash a small litter box in the back of the pet carrier for long flights. Keep disinfectant wipes and plastic poop bags in the storage section of the carrier.

7 Do not sedate your cat. Consult your vet about pet pheromone sprays or herbal remedies designed to calm a pet naturally during a stressful situation, such as flying in an aeroplane.

🐾 Make your cat's carrier inviting so she will view it as a safe haven during your travels.

Travelling by Boat

Some cats are born sailors, joining their people on boating outings and meeting other boaters at each port they visit. Help your cat earn her 'sea legs' by following these guidelines:

1 Get your cat used to water by dipping her paws in a bath or sink and then on a calm day – with your cat wearing a harness – dampen her paws in that body of water.

2 Fasten a special ID on your cat's collar. The ID should include your name, mobile number, as well as your boat's permanent marina location and slip number. Definitely have an ID microchip implanted in your cat. Include all your contact info in the form you fill out for the microchip registry agency.

3 Fit your feline with a personal flotation device. Make sure that this life vest is brightly coloured and features a handle on top to make it easier for you to retrieve should she spill in the water.

4 Be patient with a boat tour. While docked and your cat is wearing a harness, let her explore the inside of your boat. Encourage her investigation with praise and a few healthy treats.

5 Arrange for, and pack seasickness medication for your pet. Until the first voyage, you will not know if your cat is prone to motion sickness, so discuss options with your vet ahead of time.

6 Make sure your cat is aware of a carpet strip hanging off both sides of your boat for her to use to climb back up on board and position a fish net with a long handle to scoop out a cat spilled overboard.

7 Locate an anchored litter box in a place that won't spill during voyages.

8 Always carry your pet's rabies vaccination certificate and health records in a waterproof container in case you need to show proof when you dock.

CHAPTER 10
Pet First Aid

First Aid Preparation

Pets don't live in protective bubbles, but you can reduce your cat's risk for injuries and medical emergencies by taking a proactive, preventive stance with first aid.

Knowing how to stabilise and immobilise your cat in a pet emergency so you can get him safely to your vet is worth far more than showering your pet with organic catnip-filled mice, designer pet beds or custom-crafted cat trees. As well as the advice listed here, give your pet a priceless gift by enrolling in a pet first-aid class where you will learn what to do – and more importantly, what not to do – in a pet emergency when minutes count.

Lifesaving Actions and Attitudes

Following these guidelines will make sure that when a calamity occurs, you know how to react and transport your cat safely to a vet.

1 KNOW WHAT'S NORMAL FOR YOUR CAT.
Once a month, perform a thorough head-to-tail health assessment of your cat. By looking, listening and smelling, you can often catch early signs of illness or injury that could be treated more completely and less expensively by a veterinary surgeon. The added bonus is that your cat becomes more comfortable when being touched, making him more cooperative around vets, pet sitters, groomers and other pet professionals.

2 THINK BEFORE YOU APPROACH.
Resist rushing up to your feline because you risk being bitten. Instead, stop, take a deep breath in and exhale to gather yourself, then survey the scene to make sure you are safe.

3 PRACTISE PLAYFUL MUZZLING SESSIONS.
When your feline is fine and content, use treats and praise as you hone your skills on wrapping him in a bath towel or putting on a safety muzzle. Remember, that even the sweetest kitty in the world can bite and claw you when injured and in pain. By practising the proper way to safely restrain your cat when he is healthy, you gain confidence and your pet makes a positive association of the restraint with a tasty reward.

4 DON'T PANIC!
Pets tap into our emotional moods and that is why it is vital not to scream or rush up to your injured cat who may be in pain, especially if he is choking. Your emotional outburst could cause your cat to try to flee or hide under a bed or rush to swallow an item he has in his mouth and start to choke.

5 CALL YOUR VET.
Whenever possible in a pet emergency, put your phone on speaker mode and call your vet for guidance. For instance, your vet may advise you to immediately induce vomiting in your cat if he ate rat bait by using hydrogen peroxide.

By always being alert to clues in changes in your cat's health or behaviour, you can save on veterinary bills and, possibly, extend your pet's life.

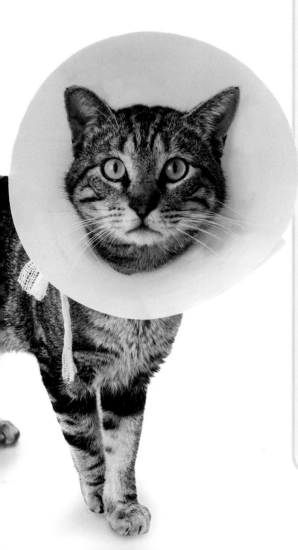

KEEP A FIRST-AID KIT

Keep a large pet first-aid kit in your home and a smaller version in your vehicle. Examine the contents twice a year and replace outdated items. Stock your kit with:

- Plastic syringe
- Tweezers
- Blunt-end scissors
- Eye dropper
- Digital thermometer
- Gauze rolls
- Gauze pads
- Triangular bandages
- Self-cling stretchy bandage
- Adhesive tape
- Pet-safe antihistamine
- Antiseptic wipes
- Hydrogen peroxide
- Chemical ice pack
- Betadine solution
- Muzzle
- Spare lead and harness
- Plastic resealable bags
- Permanent marking pen and notepad
- Towel
- Non-latex disposable gloves
- Torch
- Cotton buds/balls
- Spare sock and trainer shoe laces
- Wooden tongue depressors to splint a broken leg
- Photo of you with your cat
- Copy of your cat's medical records and veterinary contact info stored in a waterproof bag
- Emergency survival blanket
- Sterile saline solution
- Styptic powder

Towel Wrapping

Felines possess many powerful weapons in the form of their sharp claws, which slash skin, and sharp teeth, which cause deep puncture wounds. They also sport a secret weapon: a flexible spine. To keep you safe – and out of a hospital for treatment of cat scratch disease – it is imperative that you never attempt to immobilise an injured cat by scruffing him by the back of the neck. In response, he can quickly manoeuvre his flexible spine so that his back claws begin rabbit-punching your forearms, leaving you bloodied as he wiggles free and flees.

One of the most surprising must-have items in your cat's pet first-aid kit is a large towel.

For times when you need to restrain an injured cat – or trim his nails or give medication – turn to a surprising ally to make the procedure go smoothly: a large bathroom towel. Wrapping your cat in a large towel is a good way to protect yourself because you conceal his claws and prevent your cat from escaping.

Introduce the towel in a positive way. Create a positive association by placing your cat on top of a towel and then open a tin of food. Place the food on the towel so your cat has to lie or sit on the towel to eat his meal. Loosely wrap the towel over the cat's back while he eats. Gently pet his back and let him walk away when he is done eating. To wrap your cat in a 'kitty burrito' so you can safely get him inside a pet carrier and head to the veterinary clinic, follow this step-by-step guide:

1 Start with your cat several inches from the front edge of the towel and about a foot from one side.

2 Pull the front of the towel up around your cat's neck snugly so that he can't get his legs over it. Hold the ends together over the back of his neck.

3 Hold the towel together with one hand. With your free hand, wrap it over the cat.

4 Be sure to take up the slack on the side. There should be no room for your cat to squirm.

5 Wrap the other side snugly under your cat.

6 Wrap the towel around your cat again.

7 When the wrap is snug, you should be able to lift your cat by the towel and he should look comfortable.

8 If your cat wiggles to get out the back, wrap the back of the towel up and over his hind end, or cover his rear with a second towel.

PRACTICE MAKES PURR-FECT

Practise wrapping your cat in a towel when he is not injured. And, don't fret if it takes you a few tries to perfect wrapping him snugly. You will gain confidence with each wrap and should be able to reduce the time it takes for you to complete this safety manoeuvre.

Pet Emergencies

Pets don't live in protective bubbles, but you can reduce your cat's risk for injuries and medical emergencies by taking proactive, preventive measures such as learning cardiopulmonary resuscitation (CPR).

 One minute your cat could be playing with a toy mouse and the next, he could suddenly collapse and stop breathing. Or he could suffer from shock after chewing an electric cable plugged into an socket and his heart stops beating. To revive him, every minute counts. That's why knowing how to perform CPR can be a true life-saving skill.

If a pet does lose consciousness and has stopped breathing, time is of the essence. You need to take action immediately, especially if the nearest veterinary clinic is 15 or 20 minutes away. Instead of spending time to try to find a pulse to determine if a cat has a heartbeat, the latest vet-approved CPR protocols recommend immediately performing compressions on the pet's chest.

CPR

CPR consists of you performing 30 chest compressions, followed by two breaths of air from your mouth directly into your cat's nose. Repeat this 30 compressions-two-breaths-of-air sequence before checking for a pulse by placing your two middle fingers directly on your cat's femoral artery located on the inside of his back thigh near the groin. The mindset is that there is enough oxygen in the tissue and bloodstream with compressions of the chest circulating that oxygen. Also, evidence shows that every time you stop compressions, you decrease the chance of survival.

Injuries and illnesses can cause heart cessation in cats, ranging from choking on a toy, being struck by a car or suffering from a chronic heart condition.

If you witness your cat collapse and stop breathing, first collect yourself by inhaling and exhaling. This helps you not to panic and to focus on the emergency situation. Next, survey the scene to make sure it is safe to reach your cat, especially if you are outside near traffic. Then, place your cat on his side and follow these steps:

1 Place your fingers on your cat's chest in the space between his two front legs.

2 Use your fingers to compress the cat's chest one-third to one-fourth in width in a steady, quick pace for 30 counts.

3 Tilt the cat's head back to open his airway.

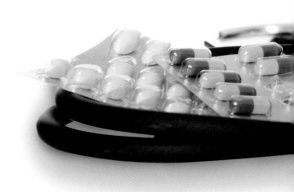

4 Gently pull his tongue forward past his canine teeth for greater airway opening.

5 Close his mouth by cupping your hands on each side of his face to form an airtight seal.

6 Give two steady breaths of air from your mouth directly into your cat's nostrils. You should see his chest rising and falling.

7 Give a second set of 30 compressions followed by two breaths of air before assessing for a heartbeat by checking for a pulse on his femoral artery.

8 Seek assistance by calling for help. Get an individual to call the nearest veterinary clinic to alert them of your arrival so that they can advise you and prepare an examination room. If you are alone, use the speaker phone option on your phone to make the call to the clinic so that you can continue to perform CPR. Certainly, there are some limitations after a pet emergency as to what an owner can do, but knowing pet first aid is very important. And, a little prevention goes a long way. Regularly pet-proof your home to keep potential dangers out of reach of your pet.

Stop the Bleeding

 If your cat steps on broken glass, catches his dewclaw in the carpet, or has his ear bitten in a catfight, expect blood to flow. Witnessing any of these scenarios can be jarring, but at times like these you need to know the steps to slow or stop the bleeding and take your cat to the nearest veterinary clinic. You have an emergency on your hands. A laceration of a large artery or vein could lead to life-threatening bleeding in minutes. The likelihood of a cat's 'bleeding out' depends on how quickly he's treated and the type of bleeding that has occurred.

THREE TYPES OF BLEEDING:

1 Arterial, characterised by spurting, bright red blood.

2 Venous, characterised by a slower flow of dark-red blood.

3 Capillary, characterised by superficial blood oozing, as could occur from a nick in the tip of the ear.

Act quickly because once a cat has lost more than 30 per cent of blood volume, he begins to develop serious shock. The first step is to protect yourself, by restraining and muzzling your cat. Keep a cat muzzle in your pet first-aid kit at home and one in your car. If your cat is bleeding from a laceration, he is likely to be in pain and even the sweetest family pet may bite if he is in pain, so it is best to be cautious and use a muzzle. Next, apply direct pressure on the wound by using sterile gauze pads from a first-aid kit. If no sterile gauze is available, a clean towel, T-shirt or any clean fabric available will work.

If blood saturates the first layer of gauze or clothing, apply another clean layer on top and apply direct pressure. Do not remove the first layer because the blood is clotting. You may need to apply several layers and direct pressure to slow or stop the bleeding. Then wrap roll gauze or fabric at least two or three times around the wound and secure it with medical tape. Be careful to make the wrap snug but not so tight that it will cut off circulation.

As soon as possible, call the nearest veterinary clinic to let them know you're on your way so that the staff can prepare a room for your cat. Ideally, have a family member or friend drive while you limit your cat's movements in the vehicle, try to keep him calm, and monitor him for signs of shock. Signs of shock include pale gums, a fast heart rate and weak pulses. Depending on the severity of the injury, your cat may be given pain medication and stitches. He may require follow-up visits for new wound dressings.

If your cat is bleeding, remember to stay calm and not panic. Your cat is depending on you to stop the bleeding and get him to a veterinary clinic for care.

The Buzz on Treating Bee Stings

Cats, even ones who live strictly indoors, are never completely safe from being stung by venomous insects. All it takes is for a wayward bee or wasp to slip through an open door or window and catch your cat's attention. His innate prey drive kicks into gear as he leaps and attempts to swat and eat the flying insect.

Most bee or wasp stings occur on a cat's front paw or face. If your cat gets stung, don't panic. In most instances, there will be mild swelling or tenderness in the area where your cat was stung. If the sting site is swollen and a little puffy, it is considered a localised reaction to the sting.

It can be tricky to determine if the swelling on your cat is due to a bee sting or other condition. But treat the symptoms as they present themselves.

For mild reactions, your first step is to try to remove the stinger as quickly as possible to slow down the spread of the venom in your cat's body. Keep in mind that the stinger can pump venom into a cat for up to 3 minutes after being separated from the bee. If the stinger is visible in the coat, use a credit card to scrape it out. Never attempt to squeeze the stinger out with tweezers because the venom sac may rupture, exposing your cat to more venom. Try to keep your cat quiet and calm and apply cool compresses to the sting site to reduce mild swelling. Run a flannel under some cool tap water; wring it out of excess water before placing it on the paw or face. Do not use icy cold compresses or ice wrapped in a towel because they can cause your cat to shiver – stick with cool compresses.

Monitor your cat and contact your local vet if the swelling grows and spreads. Most likely, the vet will advise you to give an over-the-counter antihistamine, such as Benadryl. In general, the maximum dose for cats is 1 mg per 0.5 kg (1 lb) of body weight, but find out the correct dose amount to administer to your cat from your vet.

Some over-the-counter products for people contain paracetamol a commonly used pain reliever that can be toxic to cats. In fact, cats are up to 10 times more susceptible to acetaminophen toxicity than dogs are. Others may contain cherry flavouring and are meant for children, not pets.

Some cats, just like people, are extremely allergic to insect bites. The area around the sting site may balloon in size. Within 5 to 10 minutes, their gums go from pink to white; they start vomiting; begin having difficulty breathing; start to drool; act confused and may go into anaphylactic shock. They can die if they do not receive immediate veterinary care.

Cool Advice for Burns

Even if your cat spends 24/7 indoors, he is at risk for one of three types of burns: chemical, electrical and thermal. He could be trapped in the dryer that is turned on, chew on exposed electric cable, brush up against a burning candle, or leap up on the hot surface of a ceramic cooker.

Some cats with third-degree burns may not show pain as much as those with second-degree burns. So, do not mistakenly think your cat has not been seriously burned. He needs immediate veterinary care.

Just like in people, cats can suffer first-, second- or third-degree burns. First-degree burns cause mild discomfort; second-degree burns penetrate several skin layers and are very painful; and third-degree burns injure all layers of the skin and can cause shock in your cat.

BURN GUIDELINES

1. Grab a bath towel and wrap your cat to safely restrain him and reduce your chances of being bitten or scratched. Do not wrap him too tightly in the towel because he can overheat en route to the veterinary clinic.

2. Gently place a damp cloth soaked in cool clean water on the burn site. This will act as a compress to help take away some of the heat from the burn site.

3. Call the nearest veterinary clinic to let them know you are on your way so that an examination room can be ready to treat this medical emergency.

WHAT NOT TO DO IN A BURN EMERGENCY

In case of your cat getting burned seriously, never do any of the following:

➤〉〉〉〉● Never use ice cubes on the burn site because you risk your cat developing hypothermia.

➤〉〉〉〉● Never attempt to confine your burned cat by grabbing him by the scruff, or back, of the neck. Cats have flexible spines and can quickly swivel their back legs and bite or scratch your forearms.

➤〉〉〉〉● Never apply a gauze pad or wrap on the burn site because gauze can disrupt a blister if one forms.

➤〉〉〉〉● Never pour lemon juice or vinegar to try to neutralise a chemical burn. Unintentionally, you are producing heat and causing more tissue damage.

➤〉〉〉〉● Never use over-the-counter burn ointments formulated for people on the burn site because some cats are sensitive to ingredients in products made for human use.

CHAPTER 11

Socialising

Socialising with Other Pets

Cats are creatures of habit and some take a long time in adjusting to changes in the household routine, the addition or deletion of a person or pet in the home, and even relocating furniture in the living room. Cats don't like surprises.

It truly is a cat's life for the one and only pampered feline in your home…until the day you enter the front door cradling another cat or kitten or, worse, a dog. The notion of sharing the home with another pet can cause many cats to spit up a hairball or rip up the sofa arm in protest. Or, turn your once-tame tabby into a fierce feline prizefighter.

But strong friendships can be achieved between your cat and this new two- or four-legged creature in your home. I share my home with my Furry Fab Four of two cats and two dogs. These former rescues all entered the home at different times. They have formed caring connections with one another not by chance, but because I took the time to properly – and patiently – introduce them to one another. Set your pets up for success each step of the way.

Pet-to-Pet Introductions

It's natural to want to quickly present your resident cat with the newest addition to your family. But in your excitement, don't rush them and certainly don't put them face to face immediately. Patience must be practised. No matter if your resident cat is now sharing life under your roof with another cat, dog, bird, or other pet, set everyone up for success – and possibly, the start of lifetime friendships by following this step-by-step introduction plan:

PREPARE THE GREETING ROOM.

Before bringing home the new pet, set up a 'safe' room in your house ahead of time that contains pet necessities for your newcomer. That includes toys, food and water bowls, litter box, pet bed, and perhaps a radio set on a talk show to get her used to conversations that occur in your home.

BE SNEAKY AT FIRST.

Purposely do your best to not let your resident cat see you bring in the newcomer. Whisk this new pet immediately into his temporary digs. Shut the door and play with her a bit before exiting.

WELCOME THE SNIFF GAME.

The best way to introduce your resident cat to any newcomer is not by sight, but by scent. Don't interfere or say anything when your resident cat tracks down the scent of a newcomer by sniffing under the closed door.

SPLIT YOUR PET TIME.

Devote time to each pet separately for a few days as everyone adjusts to the change in the household.

PERFORM THE TOWEL INTRODUCTION TEST.

Take a hand towel and rub it over the face and back of your resident cat. Then head into the new pet's room and do the same. And, do another round so that the towel technique successfully exchanges scents between the two of them. This is important because it is best for pets to get to know each other initially by smell. And, the toweling makes each smell a bit like the other one.

SWITCH PLACES.

After a few days or so, put the newcomer in a pet carrier and discreetly take her out of her closed room. Then put your resident cat in that room with a favourite toy and other feline amenities. After closing the door, allow your newcomer to investigate the other parts of your house, one room at a time.

PERMIT PEEKING AT MEALTIME.

Use a see-through pet door, gate or other barrier at dinner time. Allow the resident cat and newcomer to meet with this safe buffer between them while they dine.

Cats in the same household who enjoy each other's company can carry out mutual grooming and help combat loneliness when you're not home.

Cat to Cat

When you finally allow your resident cat and the new feline or kitten to meet, solicit the aid of a family member or friend to assist. Hold your resident cat in one end of the living room and have your friend hold the newcomer at the other end. Strive for a mellow meet-up by speaking quietly and by avoiding any quick movements or big gestures – all can be perceived as threats to one or both cats. Then place the cats on the floor and present each with a handful of healthy treats to enjoy in the presence of the other. Do not leave your cats unsupervised until you see them display these actions:

- Grooming in the presence of the other.
- Lying on the floor.
- Walking past one another down the hall without any hissing or swatting.
- Eating from separate food bowls in the same room without interfering with one another.

If you are not sure if your indoor cats are engageing in playful wrestling or getting ready to erupt into a full-blown claw-and-teeth fight, here's a clue: listen. Don't hear anything? Cats who play wrestle behave like feline mimes. They will do body tumbles and paw thumping without emitting any yowls or miaows. And look for these other clues that indicate this is not a real feline feud. Cats involved in play fights do not move at a fast pace. If each cat takes a turn being on her back and pouncing on her feline friend or if the pair stop and start a lot, acting like wrestlers moving on a mat to get into position, then this is equal play.

Just like dogs, cats need and deserve opportunities for physical exercise to keep their muscles toned and fend off destructive behaviour due to boredom. Cats do form selective friendships with other cats, as exhibited by mutual grooming and the occasional mock fighting.

Pay attention to any early signs of hostility between your cat and a newly adopted one. Intervene to prevent hissing from evolving into all-out cat brawls.

COMMON CAUSES OF FELINE FEUDING

Many environmental and behavioural situations can trigger a fight between two cats in your household. Here are the main triggers:

A medical problem in one of the cats.

The addition of a new pet or person to the household.

A rattling event like a broomstick crashing on the floor with Cat A blaming Cat B.

Inability to confront a trespassing cat in the backyard so displaces scorn towards the feline roommate in the home. (The animal behavioural term for this is 'redirected aggression'.)

Lack of ample feline items like water and food bowls, litter boxes and comfy perches.

A steadily simmering dislike for one another that finally escalates into feline fisticuffs.

Cat to Dog

 The truth about cats and dogs is that many form close friendships. Use that canine hierarchical mindset to your advantage. Dogs want to know clearly where they rank in the family. They don't care if they are last, even behind the pet mouse. What they don't tolerate is canine confusion caused by one family member treating them like a king – and ranking above the family cat – while another family member designates the dog at a lower ranking below the cat.

Demonstrate to your dog, in action and attitude, that the family cat outranks them. My dogs, Chipper and Cleo, definitely respect my cats, Murphy and Zeki, because I consistently feed my felines first and have my dogs sit in the 'park' position to wait for their bowls. I also keep my dogs in a 'down, stay' at the back patio door so that my cats can saunter out to my fenced backyard for supervised outings. My dogs don't exit until I say, 'Okay, let's go!' Lastly, I greet my cats first and then my dogs when I come home.

Set up your dog-cat family for success by letting them view one another initially from a distance. Keep your dog on a long lead at first so that you can step on the lead should she foolishly decide to dart after the cat. This enables you to control her playful – or predatory – lunges towards the cat. When they are both in the room, provide each of them with treats, giving first to the cat. This helps build a positive association that good things happen when they are in the same room. Other pointers are:

- Provide your cat with escape routes that cannot be accessed by your dog, such as a towering, sturdy cat tree or under a bed.
- Make sure the new pet has her own possessions.
- Never force your pets to share a food bowl or toys.
- Provide water bowls in different rooms.
- Provide your dog with plenty of vigorous walks and playtime daily so she will be a bit more tired when around the cat inside.
- Heed the hiss warning by intervening and calling your dog over to you. This is a feline's early warning sign before she plans to attack.

Many households have both cats and dogs. When introduced properly, they can enjoy lifetime friendships.

Socialising With Humans

Yes, cats do have favourite people. These people tend to be ones who communicate clearly and consistently with felines. Pay attention to your cat's body and verbal cues to improve harmony in your household.

Cat to Baby

Whether you are a new mum or preparing your home for houseguests who are bringing a baby or toddler, you can make steps to protect the baby and minimise any level of stress in your cat.

KEEP YOUR CAT OUT OF THE BABY'S ROOM.

It is a myth that cats 'suck' the breath out of babies. The real attraction for a curious cat is the feel of the warm, soft crib and the sweet-smelling milk breath from the baby. The solution is to keep your cat in another room, keep the baby's room closed, or place a cat net over the crib.

KEEP YOUR CAT'S NAILS TRIMMED.

Or consult your vet about fitting your feline with a product such as Soft Claws, which are tiny plastic caps for cat nails (see page 53).

Most cats do not like being rushed up to and given enthusiastic greetings that consist of hearty hugs and hellos.

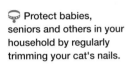 **Protect babies, seniors and others in your household by regularly trimming your cat's nails.**

Cat to Spouse or Guests

Ranking high on the list of pet peeves among cats is being on the receiving end of forced hugs and greetings. It is easy to be guilty of committing this major cat sin. For many cat lovers who return home after a business trip, holiday or simply a long workday, they tend to burst through the door, chase down their cats, and engage in a big group hug. No surprise that your cats react by wiggling free and racing away. Once you calm down and sit on the sofa, magically, your cats will slowly approach and greet you on their own terms.

Accept this fact that the more you try to force affection on your cats, the less they want to give you. Not all cats are lap cats or want to be held tightly and cuddled. Being overly affectionate can actually drive your cats from you. Play hard to get. In other words, act more like a cat, pretend not to care and your cats will seek you out for attention and affection. This advice applies to cat-adoring guests who need to take a cue from people who are allergic to or who don't like cats: avoid direct eye contact, sit or stand still, and do not say a word to the cat. A confident cat will be happy to make the first move by sauntering your way and rubbing his body against your leg or granting you permission to scratch his chin or run your hand across his back. Cultivate a true bond with a cat and you will have a feline friend for life. Finally, make sure your cat has a safe room or safe place to escape to when she wants to get away from overly animated guests.

Socialising with Prey

If you wish to share your home – and heart – with cats and their natural prey, such as birds or mice, you need to be vigilant in protecting these smaller pets from your feline.

Cats and Birds and/or Mouse

Even though your tabby can count on you providing her with nutritious meals, she still may be tempted to unleash her instinctive predatory nature towards the family bird or mouse. So, even if your cat seems blasé around these small creatures, never leave them unsupervised. Always make sure that the bird or mouse is tucked safely in its cage out of access from your cat.

Separate them if your cat stares fixedly at the bird or mouse, folds his ears back and begins to twitch his tail (a behaviour usually performed right before pouncing on a prey), or makes a distinctive chirping or cackling sound at the sight of the family bird. That said, some cats do tone down their predatory natures and become buddies with birds and mice.

So if you desire to have a home filled with wings and fur, take extra precautions to keep birds and mice safe at all times.

Divert your cat's prey-minded tendencies towards pet birds and mice by engageing them in play sessions with wand toys and wind-up toys.

IS YOUR CAT A THERAPY CAT CANDIDATE?

Never underestimate the power of the purr. In addition to dogs, well-socialised therapy cats are visiting in greater numbers at care homes, hospitals and schools. They provide residents, patients, students and staff with many health benefits. Among my favourite pluses therapy cats offer:

Therapy cats aid in improving fine motor skills in nursing home residents, who may be more motivated to open a jar to retrieve a treat to feed the visiting cat or use their hand to pet the cat from the top of the head to the base of the tail.

Therapy cats encourage children with special needs, like autism or behaviour disorders, to improve their communication skills by 'speaking' with these trained cats.

Therapy cats elevate moods for people coping with anxiety issues or depression.

Therapy cats provide unconditional, uncomplicated friendship. During their visits, they don't have any hidden agendas or demands. They don't judge those they visit.

Do you think your cat has the temperament to qualify as a therapy pet? The best therapy cats are friendly, outgoing and confident. It is as if they have never met a stranger or been in a strange place. It is likely that some level of assessment will be required, so it is best to research and check these terms with your nearest pets as therapy organisation.

Schedule times when you can let your pet bird or mouse safely out of its cage by ushering your prey-minded cat into another, closed room.

CHAPTER 12

Budgeting

Money Matters

The unconditional love and devotion pets give us can't be measured by any monetary value, but it is nonetheless imperative to be smart with how we spend our hard-earned cash.

People all over the globe are searching for ways to s-t-r-e-t-c-h the family budget – and that includes expenses doled out for pets. Here are money-saving tactics guaranteed not to shortchange the quality of life for your cat:

INVEST IN QUALITY, COMMERCIAL PET FOOD.

Select pet food that lists a real meat as the first ingredient – not maize or wheat. Doing so can keep your pet healthy and that translates into fewer vet bills to deal with pancreatitis, diabetes and a host of other health conditions. Don't forget to sniff out discount coupons or contact your favourite pet manufacturer and request coupons.

BRING OUT YOUR PET CHEF SKILLS.

Keep more money in your wallet by making healthy homemade treats in a large enough batch that you can store the extras in the freezer. You can use top-quality ingredients, but they will cost less because you're not paying for packageing and marketing and shipping.

ONLY USE CAT TOOTHPASTES AND BRUSHES.

Brush your cat's teeth at least two times a week, using toothpastes and brushes designed for pets. These at-home dental items are minor in cost compared to a professional dental cleaning performed at a veterinary clinic.

PACKAGE THE NECESSARY VACCINATIONS.

Consult your vet about what vaccinations your cat truly needs and base it on your pet's age, health, and outdoor access. Opt for 3-year vaccinations, if these are available, instead of annual ones.

GET STORE BARGAINS.

Save a few pence to a few pounds by buying litter, leads, bowls, bed and treats at places that primarily cater to two-leggers, such as major discount stores and supermarkets rather than pet shops or pet boutiques.

BUY IN BULK.

Look for treats and chews from online pet supply catalogues and store them in the freezer. For dry food, you shouldn't really buy too much in bulk, but if you do then store it inside airtight containers to keep it fresh.

SHOP AROUND AND THEN BARTER.

If a catalogue has a low price on heartworm pills or flea treatment, ask if your vet will match it.

FORM A BUYING CO-OP WITH FRIENDS.

Lots of catalogues offer a discounted bulk price for large group orders.

TRADE YOUR SERVICES.

If you have a particular skill – such as writing, painting, making pottery, mowing, gardening, or car valeting – consider offering your talents in trade for pet services.

WHAT NEVER TO CUT OUT

Just remember: full-throttle cat purrs are always free. Pets bring out the best in us, especially during tough economic times. You might lack a few of the luxuries in life, but you're never poor as long as you have the love of your dog or cat.

So, invest in your cat's health by maintaining twice-a-year vet examinations for him. These visits will help your vet catch conditions during their early stages where treatment can be less expensive and there is a greater chance for a full recovery. The sooner problems are detected, the better the prognosis for your cat.

RESIST CHOOSING LOW-COST CAT LITTERS.

These so-called bargains can produce more dust, which can impact your cat's respiratory system.

WORK THE WEB.

Consider purchasing cat carriers, leads and food bowls at car boot sales or go on websites like Gumtree to purchase new pet items for a fraction of what they sell for at retail prices. In these tough economic times, there are ways you can stretch your money and still ensure your cat is healthy and happy.

Whittle Down Pet Expenses from the Start

Owning a cat does not have to be as expensive as some people believe. You can be clever with your money and ensure your cat lives a happy, healthy life.

ADOPT A CAT FROM YOUR LOCAL SHELTER.

Rather than purchasing a pet from a shop or breeder, why not adopt from an animal shelter? Shelter pets are significantly less expensive, and you are saving an animal's life in the process. Often, too, the shelter's nominal adoption fee ensures that your pet has been altered and vaccinated, saving you from these charges at the veterinary clinic.

ENROLL IN A PET FIRST-AID CLASS.

You can learn ways to protect your cat and what to do, and not to do, in a pet emergency when minutes count.

BECOME YOUR CAT'S PERSONAL STYLIST.

Invest in quality nail clippers, brushes and shampoos and learn how to groom, bathe, trim nails and administer flea and tick preventive medicines properly. By regularly grooming your cat, you can prevent matted fur from developing.

Don't Scrimp when Buying Medication

Although some owners might look to save money by administering human medications that they already have on hand to their cats, vets strongly recommend against it. Many human medications, including paracetamol, aspirin, and ibuprofen are toxic to cats.

Because cats metabolise things differently than humans, medications that work for humans won't necessarily work for cats. On the other hand, low-cost generic medications made for cats are perfectly fine. Consult your vet.

The cost to properly care for your cat can add up quickly if you don't exercise frugal spending habits.

Routinely, inspect each room of your house to identify possible items that could cause injury to your cat or other family pet.

Save Money by Pet-Proofing Your Home

A bit of accident prevention can save you a lot of money. To reduce the risk of injury-causing accidents, take a good look around your house. Unfortunately, things most attractive to cats can often be the most hazardous.

The idea of a kitten playing with a ball of yarn may sound sweet, but it is very dangerous. If ingested, long strings can become entangled in the cat's intestinal tract, causing severe damage.

Strings, wool, thin rubber bands and tinsel do not belong in a house with cats. Other potentially risky items include beads, marbles, buttons, needles, pins, tacks, and discarded dental floss in bathroom rubbish bins, as well as plastic bags, which can cause suffocation or intestinal blockages if swallowed. Cat-proof your home by stashing these items in drawers, cabinets, inside storage boxes with lids, or litter bins with lids.

Homemade Toys

Before you spend money on commercial cat toys, reconsider items already inside your home that can provide your cat with a lot of playtime fun.

 Making toys for your cat helps to curb your spending and is also a great personal or family project.

SCRATCHING POST

Commercial scratching posts available at pet shops can be expensive. Instead, visit your local hardware and carpet store to gather what you need to make a customised number for your feline.

YOU WILL NEED:

Sandpaper
Thick plywood, at least 60 m (24 in) square
Soft marking pencil
Thick, round closet rod (wooden dowel), 45 cm (18 in) in length
2 sturdy angle irons with fitting screws
Small power drill
Screwdriver
Small carpet remnant
Contact adhesive
Paper cement
Heavy hemp rope or sisal
Nails
Hammer

1 Sand and smooth out the edges of the plywood to remove all splinters.

2 Mark the centre of the plywood using a pencil and place the dowel upright there.

3 Position the angle irons on opposite sides of the dowel. Use a pencil to mark the screw holes on the dowel and the board.

4 Drill small holes to start the screws and then screw the angle irons tightly in place.

5 Cover the board with a small piece of carpet remnant, gluing firmly in place.

6 Apply paper cement to the dowel, beginning at the bottom. Work on small areas at a time.

7 Once the cement has dried, cover in glue and wrap the dowel tightly with heavy hemp rope or sisal, pushing each spiral close to the previous one. Add more glue to the post as you work upwards.

8 Finish the top with a tight single knot and use a hammer to nail in place, so the knot is on the top of the post. (Care must be taken to pound the nails completely in so the nail head is flush with the wood.) Cut the rope a few inches above the knot and unravel the end to make a stiff brush-like tassel.

QUICK-FIX TOYS

If time is a factor, why not keep it simple and try some of these recycled homemade toys.

Toss a plastic bottle cap into an empty bath and watch your cat go after it, knocking the cap around like a hockey puck.

Cut holes in a plastic water bottle, small enough to dispense kibble when the cat rolls the bottle around.

Scrunch up aluminium foil or paper into a ball and toss it down the hall, over the sofa, or up the stairs for your cat to fetch.

Tether strips of fabric together and then snake it across the floor for your cat to pounce upon.

Stuff catnip and crumpled cellophane in a sock. Knot the top so your cat can paw it.

KITTY TETHERBALL

Cats can't resist objects that move up and down and erratically, but some commercial toys can be pricey. Save some pennies by reaching for your toolbox and some inexpensive materials and watch your cat swat at your creation like a prizefighter.

YOU WILL NEED:
Fabric
Cotton wadding
22-gauge steel wire
Wire cutters
Heavy-duty thread
Needle
Large plastic clip
Needle-nose pliers

INSTRUCTIONS:

1 Fashion a fabric ball about the size of a baseball and stuff it with cotton wadding.

2 Cut a 1 m (3 ft) length of steel wire. Use the needle and heavy-duty thread to sew one end of the wire to the fabric ball. Slip the other end of the wire through the hold of the large plastic clip.

3 Use needle-nose pliers to fasten the wire securely and to tuck in the wire ends.

4 Connect the clip with the wired ball attached to an opened door jamb or to the edge of a sturdy piece of furniture. Adjust the height to ensure the wired ball moves without touching the floor to motivate your cat to investigate and give it a swat.

Pet Insurance

How financially prepared are you to cover a costly veterinary bill? Where will the money come from? Pet insurance is especially important for pet owners on a budget.

Veterinary medicine advances, such as high-tech tools and disease-fighting remedies, are keeping pets healthy longer, but paying for those advances can take a big bite out of your wallet. Insurance is essential for those who want to offer their pets medical treatments such as chemotherapy, but can't afford the out-of-pocket costs.

Pros and Cons of Pet Insurance

In deciding if pet insurance is your best option, be aware that coverage plans vary widely among pet insurance companies. Keep in mind that there really is no best pet insurance company. The better question you need to ask is, 'Which pet insurance company is the best one to insure my pet?' It is equally important to recognise if pet insurance really won't benefit your situation – say, if you adopt senior pets or adult pets with special needs or enjoy having a house full of cats and dogs. If you fall into any of those scenarios, your best option may be to dedicate a credit card for pet expenses or talk to your vet before a costly calamity strikes to work out a payment plan option. Here are some insights to help you pick the right plan for your pet:

ASSESS THE LEVEL OF COVERAGE.
Select a plan based on the coverage it provides and not solely on its price. The least expensive plan may provide the least amount of coverage.

BUY WHEN YOU FIRST GET YOUR CAT.
Don't wait to purchase pet insurance until after your pet gets sick. Some plans do not cover pre-existing conditions.

IT IS EASIER TO DOWNGRADE A POLICY.
Get the best policy you can afford on the front end, because it is easier to downgrade rather than attempt to upgrade as your pet ages. Adding policies such as dental and wellness are more expensive if you delay in obtaining them until your pet hits middle age.

MULTI-PET DISCOUNTS ARE POSSIBLE.
Find out if the company offers discounts for coverage of two or more pets.

PERCENTAGE PLANS ARE BEST.
Since the cost for a veterinary procedure can vary from one veterinary clinic to the next, choose a policy that reimburses based on a percentage of the veterinary bill instead of offering a set amount for a condition.

READ THE FINE PRINT.
Look for any hidden deductions in the policy contract, such as not covering examiantion fees, first-day hospitalisation costs, or paying less (higher co-payment) for emergency visits or specialists care.

WHAT IS THE PAYMENT CAP?
Find out ahead of time if the plan carries a payment cap per incident, per year or per the lifetime of the pet.

INSURANCE GLOBALLY
How well pet insurance is embraced depends on geography. Pet insurance has been available in Europe since the late 1940s, whereas it is relatively new in the United States, with the first policy not sold until 1982. In fact, only 3 per cent of Americans with pets have pet insurance as compared to 25 per cent of people with pets in Great Britain and 49 per cent in Sweden. The reason appears to be that people in Europe have grown up with pet insurance for generations and it is far more accessible.

CHAPTER 13

The Early Years

Kittenhood Care

The first year of a kitten's life can be fascinating and frustrating for both you and your young cat. Kittens aren't born with instant manners or training manuals. Leaping, pouncing, climbing and diving are built into their genetic code so they require lots of time, attention and training. Each day is a new adventure.

Kittens seem to possess an innate ability to create mayhem, mischief and madness – all in the name of feline fun. After coping with their endless energy, chewing and clawing, you wonder why you took on such a time-demanding task. These supercharged, high-energy kittens spend their waking hours vigorously exploring their environments and testing their abilities, and your patience.

Pet-proofing the home is a must to keep electric cables, chocolate, household cleaners and the kitchen rubbish can out of paw's reach. Be prepared for those surprise toe-attacks while you snooze by your young feline, who is honing her hunting skills in the pre-dawn hours. Here are key kitten-training tactics designed to help you survive the 'wonder year' and maintain your sanity:

START BEHAVIOUR TRAINING ON DAY 1.

Don't delay. Kittens grow up fast and you don't want bad habits to become permanent ones. Never reward bad behaviour, even when it is cute.

ENROLL IN A KITTEN CLASS.

Puppy classes are well known, but until recently, such classes were unheard of for kittens. Kitty training classes may be available in your area and will hopefully focus on accomplishing two goals: socialising the kittens and helping people better understand why felines do what they do. The kittens learn to be handled, groomed and examined and to explore new places with confidence. Contact your local vet or animal shelter in case a kitten class is organised nearby or seek an online course with help from your vet.

USE CONSISTENT COMMANDS AND GESTURES.

Always use the same voice commands and hand gestures so you don't confuse your kitten. For instance, always say, 'Sit up' and raise your index finger when you want your feline student to stretch up with her weight resting on her hind feet.

AVOID PHYSICAL PUNISHMENT.

Your hand should be viewed as a friend, not a foe to your kitten. Hitting a kitten fosters fear and distrust. You need to be regarded as the benevolent leader, the keeper of all good resources (and that includes high-quality treats).

REMEMBER THE SPECIES.

You adopted a kitten, not a puppy. The two species have different motivations for what they do. Don't expect your kitten to fetch your slippers. Whereas a puppy often strives to please you, a more independent-minded kitten needs to know what's in it for her before she will comply.

CUSTOMISE YOUR BEHAVIOUR TRAINING.

If you have adopted more than one kitten, recognise that each may have a different personality – even if they are littermates. Strive to meet the individuality of each kitten during your mini-training sessions and keep in mind that some kittens respond to some techniques better than others.

ESSENTIAL KITTEN KIT

Congratulations on the adoption of your new kitten! Before she steps her first paw in your door, make sure you acquire these items:

- Kitten food
- Litter box
- Litter
- Food and water bowls
- Breakaway collar and identification tag
- Carrier
- Sturdy scratching post or pad
- Fabric window perch
- Comfy bed or big soft pillows for catnapping
- Nail clippers
- Toys
- Brush/comb
- Feline shampoo

Monthly Progress Report

During the first year of your kitten's life, she seems to grow literally right in front of your eyes! She is developing mentally and physically at an amazing rate. Your fast-growing kitten will experience a 2,000 per cent increase in her birth weight during her first 5 months. She will be 95 per cent adult-like in physical size, intelligence and attitude by her first birthday. Let's look at what to expect when it comes to physical and mental developments for your kitten with the following key milestones:

BIRTH TO THE FIRST MONTH.

A newborn kitten cannot see or hear for the first 2 weeks and must rely on the senses of touch and taste. The momma cat serves as chief chef, source of warmth and clean-up crew (tidying up her litter's urine and faeces deposits). By age 3 weeks, a kitten starts to realise there is a world out there beyond her mother. Littermates begin to vie for rank and turf. By 4 weeks, baby teeth start poking through the gums.

BY 8 WEEKS.

Physically, a kitten can now tap all 5 senses. She has learned to emit high-pitched shrieks when her littermates nip too harshly during play as they learn how to inhibit their bites. She has developed eye-paw coordination to swat at toys and her neuromuscular system is strong enough for her to start using a litter box. She should be completely weaned from her mother and able to eat kibble. Kittens at this age also start to groom themselves. They also develop social interaction skills and sleeping patterns.

BY 7 MONTHS.

It may surprise you to learn, but most kittens reach their physical size (in terms of height) by 6 months of age. All of a kitten's permanent teeth are coming in, which explains a kitten's need to chew to relieve gum discomfort. A 7-month-old kitten can enter her first heat cycle and become pregnant. An intact male kitten's sexual hormones are also fully developed to enable him to mate. Mentally, a kitten at this age is starting to flex her independence and desire to explore her surroundings solo. This time marks the most active play period in kittenhood. This young feline will start to scoop, toss, paw, mouth, and hold objects and initiate tail-chasing, leaping, dancing and pouncing as she determines her ranking in the household – compared to you and other pets.

BY 12 MONTHS.

By a kitten's first birthday, she should be 95 per cent adult-like in physical size, intelligence and attitude. A 1-year-old cat is the human equivalent of a 15-year-old teenager in terms of mental development. Welcome to the age of feline adolescence as your 'teenage' kitten begins to challenge the household rules and try to test how far she can push the limits (such as rudely waking you up an hour before your alarm clock sounds).

FELINE LIFE STAGES

The domesticated cat sports 4 stages in life that may vary slightly by breed:

- GROWTH: birth to 1 year
- YOUNG ADULT: 1 to 7 years
- MATURE ADULT: 7 to 12 years
- GERIATRIC: 12 years and older

KEEPING KITTEN HEALTHY

Kittens who are petted, cuddled and touched by people 15 to 40 minutes a day during their first 7 weeks of life are more apt to grow up to be playful, better students and well-socialised. Kittens also require twice as many calories per pound of body weight than adult cats. Check the label of your commercial food bag or tin for specific serving portions based on your feline's age, health status and activity level. Lastly, it may be wise to invest early on and consider purchasing pet health insurance for your new kitten or cat. Insurance premiums cost the least when your feline is young and healthy. Insurance plans help offset emergency veterinary visits or expensive treatment for serious health issues such as diabetes or hyperthyroidism.

Think Like a Mama Cat

 Too often, owners learn as they go – and as their kittens grow. To help you survive kittenhood and develop a strong bond that lasts a lifetime, you can pick up a lot of pointers from your kitten's mum. Whether the mother cat is present or absent, here are insider tips on caring for kittens:

INTENTIONALLY DISH UP DIFFERENT CHOW.

By offering a variety of quality commercial kitten dry foods in different shapes, textures and flavours, you lessen your kitten's chance of growing up to be a finicky eater. Kittens fed only one kind of food during the socialisation period of 4 to 7 weeks may be imprinted to the point that they decide this is food and anything else is not acceptable.

REACT OBVIOUSLY TO MISBEHAVIOUR.

Learn to hiss and say ouch in a loud tone when your kitten misbehaves to teach her manners. If your overly energised kitten bites you or scratches you during play, say 'Ow!' very loudly, look at her, and hiss and then leave the room to tell her that she is not fun to play with. The wrong action is to act stoic, which gives no feedback to your kitten.

RESIST PLAY USING YOUR HANDS OR TOES.

You may think it is cute for an 8-week-old kitten to play fight with your hand, but you are unintentionally creating a biter. Everyone in the household needs to comply with this no-hands play rule. Instead, use wand toys and feather toys when playing with your kitten and let her understand that hands are for stroking and scratching behind the ears and not for rough play.

GIVE HEAD-TO-TAIL WELLNESS ASSESSMENTS.

Touch your kitten gently and get her used to having her ears, mouth, paws and belly touched daily. This will increase the chances of her being a calmer feline during a veterinary exam.

LOCATE THE LITTER BOX IN A KITTEN-SAFE PATH.

Make sure the litter box is located in an area out of household foot traffic and away from noisy appliances. Bring your young kitten to the litter box. Scoop out the deposits daily and make sure that the litter is about 75 mm (3 in) deep.

MAKE SCRATCH-FRIENDLY AREAS.

To stop kittens from scratching your furniture with their razor-sharp claws, you need to redirect your young cat's attention to something you want her to use, like a sturdy scratching post.

KEEP YOUR KITTEN COZY.

Felines under the age of 1 possess a greater need for warmth than a mature cat. If you don't have a pet-safe heating pad, try placing dry rice in a thick, white sports sock in the microwave for 1 minute. Be sure to knot the end of the sock closed. This rice-filled sock will stay warm for a couple hours.

Engage in Cat Chat

Make your new kitten feel right at home by greeting her by name and speaking in soothing, flattering tones. She may not understand people-talk, but she will begin to recognise her name, and more importantly, learn to associate hearing your voice with all things pleasant and positive. As silly as it may sound, even try mewing back at her once in a while. Your kitten will appreciate your most feeble attempt at cat chat.

Select Safe Toys

It can be fun to shop for toys for your young cat, but avoid selecting any kitten toys with sewn-on bells, eyes or buttons. These small items can pose a choking hazard in the paws (and mouths) of a play-minded kitten. Some furry mice have dart-like eyes, which can come out and puncture an intestine.

Another safety consideration is to beware of strings. Dutifully dispose of wool, dental floss, sewing thread, Christmas tree tinsel and even the string used on beef roasts in containers unable to be accessed by curious kittens. A kitten can strangle on these stringy items and if ingested, they can cause possible fatal internal injuries. Toys with strings can evoke great fun, but introduce them to your kitten during your supervision and put them away when you are not around. Pick up all the little things on the floor – especially items like rubber bands, string, sewing pins. Because of the barbs in the back of their mouths, cats can't spit things out.

A kitten does a lot of physical and mental growing in his first year and relies on you as his surrogate parent for guidance.

Play with Your Kitten

Devote 10 minutes once or twice a day to engage in fun games with your kitten and you will reap a multitude of benefits. You help your young cat to develop a fun-loving, friendly personality as well as bolster her self-confidence. Another health benefit is that her muscle tone and coordination will develop. As well as minimising your kitten's fear of meeting new people or other pets, you strengthen the bond between you and your kitten for a friendship that will last a lifetime.

The upshot is that you need to play creative games with your kitten. Sure, expensive shop-bought cat games can meet your kitten's need to work her muscles and her brainpower. But you and your kitten can have oodles of fun by using some common household items. All you need to do is unleash your creativity. Consider these low-cost feline games:

PURSUE THE SHOELACE

Take a long shoelace, tie a toy mouse to one end and hold the other end in your hand. Call your kitten by name and once you catch her attention, race up and down your hallway with the toy mouse dragging across the floor.

Zoom right past your attentive kitten, who will find this moving mouse to be irresistible and will give chase. Once she has perfected the long hallway chase, expand to add twists and turns by dragging the shoelace-mouse toy in and out of rooms. Continually call out your kitten's name and praise her for every successful mouse pounce. Both of you will get a great workout!

A pair of kittens can enjoy plenty of playtime together, but young felines need and deserve interaction with you during daily play sessions.

KITTY IN THE MIDDLE

This is the ideal game to play if you have an acrobatic kitten who loves to leap and grab at objects in mid-air. You will need another person to play this game.

Place your kitten in the middle of the room. Have you and your friend sit about 3.5 m (12 ft) apart on either end. Hold a toy mouse or crinkle a paper wad to get your kitten's attention. Now, loft the mouse or paper wad so it just barely clears your kitten's head. Toss it back and forth a few times and watch your kitten gear up to leap and snap this airborne object. Each time she 'scores', be sure to praise her in upbeat tones. Continue the tossing until she stops to groom or walks away. It is the universal feline sign that the game is over.

GO FISHING

Kittens can't seem to fight the temptation to explore a paper bag left on the floor. In no time, they are leaping inside and then poking out their heads to survey the scene. Jazz up this natural instinct by having your kitten play a game of 'land fishing'.

First, snip off the handles of a paper shopping bag to keep her from getting tangled and also cut a large circle in the bottom of the bag. Now, fasten a toy mouse to the end of a long sneaker shoelace – that is your fishing reel.

Place the bag on the floor on its side with the bottom end facing you. Insert the toy mouse through the circular opening until it reaches about midway inside the bag. Call your kitten over or position her so that she is looking at the open front end of the bag.

Now, wiggle the toy mouse inside the bag and encourage her to dive inside to capture this 'prey'. As she flies inside the bag, reel the toy mouse out of the circular hole. Repeat these steps and always praise her for her savvy hunting skills.

FELINE HOCKEY

Harness your kitten's speed and ability to turn on a penny. Usher her to your empty bath. Toss a paper wad, ping-pong ball or lightweight plastic golf ball inside the bath and watch her perform like a four-legged hockey star in this confined game of chase.

Safety Check Your Home

Before your kitten is introduced to her new surroundings, spend some time kitty-proofing your home. That means going room to room and actually getting on all fours so you can view the interior from a feline's perspective. Don't forget to look up high because kittens are climbers and love to view their 'world' from a lofty perch, such as the top of your living room curtains or the refrigerator.

Kittens are inquisitive by nature, so it is up to us to keep breakable family heirlooms out of paw's reach. Here are some kitty-proofing ideas:

* Place childproof latches on doors housing rubbish, medicines, household cleaners or other no-feline-allowed items.
* Wrap or cover curtain or blind cords to prevent accidental choking.
* Avoid stacking books or magazines on a coffee table or high shelf where they can topple under the weight of a kitten who leaps up and then loses her footing.
* Secure precious breakable items inside glass cabinets with latches.
* Avoid plants that can be poisonous for your kitten. Among the ones that can make your kitten sick if ingested are Easter lilies, aloe vera, daffodils, hyacinths, oleander, poinsettia and tulips.
* Keep toilet lids down to prevent your kitten from drinking out of the basin, which can harbour bacteria and harmful cleaning chemicals.
* Insert exposed electric cables in chew-resistant casings available at hardware or pet shops. Chewing live wires can cause mouth burns or, worse, electrocution. You can also try spritzing the cords with smells felines hate: hair spray, citrus-scented sprays, bitter apple or cayenne pepper.

Despite their small size, kittens are capable of getting into big trouble unless you properly pet-proof your home interior.

Meet the Vet

Your young kitten will need to make several veterinary visits for checkups and vaccinations during her first year. To prime her for what to expect, regularly open her mouth, lightly press on each footpad, touch her from head to tail and do a 'mock' at-home examination by placing her on top of your washing machine, which mimics the slickness and height of most stainless steel veterinary examination tables.

Consult your vet about what vaccinations your kitten needs to stay healthy. There are core and non-core vaccines and your vet can advise you on which ones are appropriate for your kitten based on her health, activity level, and if she interacts with other pets or travels. Vaccines are administered to protect your kitten from many diseases, including:

- Rabies
- Feline leukemia virus (FeLV)
- Feline infectious peritonitis (FIP)
- Ringworm
- Feline distemper

Neutering

A pair of mating cats plus their offspring can produce more than 750,000 cats in just 7 years! Do your part to help combat pet overpopulation by booking an appointment to have your kitten spayed or neutered. With medical advances, these surgical procedures can be safely done on kittens as young as 8 weeks of age who weigh at least 11 kg (2 lb). There are many good reasons:

- Altered cats, on average, live longer, healthier lives than intact felines.
- Neutered males are less tempted to roam and get into cat fights.
- Spayed females are at less risk for developing ovarian or breast cancer or uterine infections.
- Neutered males are less prone to develop prostate cancer.
- Altered males are less likely to urine-mark on your furniture.
- Intact females can go into heat as young as 5 months of age and yowl incessantly.

Get your kitten used to being handled as he would in a veterinary clinic by doing 'mock' at-home examinations.

CHAPTER 14

The
Senior
Years

Ageless Tips for Senior Cats

Old age is not a disease, it is simply a stage in life. It is far easier to spot signs of ageing in dogs with their noticeable greying muzzles, but it can be more challenging in cats because their signs are often more subtle.

It's easy to overlook that your senior feline catnaps on the carpeted floor instead of on the top ledge of his cat tower. Or, you may not give a second thought to filling the water bowls more often or scooping larger-sized urine clumps from the litter box. But inside their bodies, a lot of hidden ageing is taking place. Their metabolism slows down and bone density lessens. Many senior cats silently suffer the painful effects of osteoarthritis or have diabetes, heart issues or failing kidneys.

Thanks to advances in veterinary medicine, improved commercial diets and a stronger people-pet connection, our cats are living longer. And that is to be celebrated. Many of us are sharing our homes – and hearts – with senior pets. In fact, one-third of all cats are at least 7 years old. Depending on the breed, that equates to senior citizenship status.

PLAY PET DETECTIVE AND LOOK FOR AGE-CHANGING CLUES.

Once a week, perform a head-to-tail assessment of your cat. Sniff inside his ears and mouth, palpate his abdomen and run your fingers through his coat. Alert your vet if you detect foul breath, lumps, nasal discharge or if your pet hesitates going up stairs or seems to struggle to walk into the litter box.

BOOK TWICE-A-YEAR SENIOR HEALTH VETERINARY EXAMS.

As your cat exits middle age, ageing accelerates. Prolong his quality of life and, possibly, catch and treat conditions early by scheduling a senior veterinary examination every 6 months. Recommended senior tests include a thorough physical examination, complete blood-count screening, urinalysis,

faecal examinations, blood-chemistry panel, parasite evaluation and, if warranted, X-rays and an ultrasound. These age-related checks aid your vet in catching conditions possibly at the onset when they can be better treated and often at a financial saving to you.

TURN MEALTIME INTO A HUNTING ADVENTURE.

Keep your cat's mind sharp by going bowl-less on occasion and hiding pieces of kibble in a room for him to find or stashing kibble inside a food puzzle toy for him to nose or swat out. Recognise that as your cat ages, his nutrition also needs to change. After all, your senior cat will have different nutritional needs than when he was a kitten. Work with your vet on a diet that best suits your senior feline's needs.

FLOOR YOUR PET WITH SURE-FOOTED DECOR.

Install rubber mats near feeding stations and rug runners on wood or tile hallways to provide traction and reduce the chance of your cat slipping and falling.

STEP UP THE SNOOZING COMFORT.

Older pets spend more time snoozing – up to 16 hours a day. Treat them to cushioned, egg-crate-type padding beds and pet-safe heating elements to soothe their arthritic joints, especially during cold months.

Take note if your senior cat is sleeping more than normal. It could be a subtle sign of a health issue that needs to be addressed by a veterinary surgeon.

Pet-proof Your Home, a Second Time

Think back a decade or more ago when you first brought home your then-curious kitten and how dutifully you made your home safe. It's time to pet-proof your home again, this time with a senior-cat safety theme.

Remember installing doorway gates and childproof latches on cabinets for your kitten? It's time to revise your approach for your aged cat:

- Provide a low-level litter box on each level of your home to make them easier for your senior cat to enter and exit.
- Swap out the old cat beds with orthopedic pet beds designed to cushion joints.
- Turn on pet-safe heating pads set on low during cold temperatures to improve blood flow and circulation in their arthritic bodies.
- Older cats are at greater risk for arthritis and mobility issues. They may need easy-to-climb ramps to get up and down your sofa and bed or safely access a sturdy cat tree.
- Elevate food and water bowls to ward off any neck strain for your senior cat to stay nourished. Replace deep food bowls with a plate.
- If you smoke, stop. Research conducted at leading veterinary universities confirms that there is a direct correlation between people smoking in the home and an increased risk of cancer in their cats. A cat grooming his coat is in fact ingesting nicotine and other cigarette toxins.

FOOD FOR THOUGHT FOR YOUR SENIOR CAT

Don't be fooled by the label 'senior' on commercial dog and cat food packages. There is no legal meaning for senior pet food – it is a marketing term. Instead, work closely with your vet to select food that matches your ageing pet's activity level, breed and health condition. For example, some senior cats may be contending with brain changes that lessen their appetite. Re-spark their interest at mealtimes by warming their food in the microwave for a few seconds to release the aroma and/or add salt-free chicken soup to their dry food.

Teach an Old Cat New Tricks

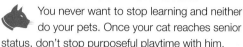 You never want to stop learning and neither do your pets. Once your cat reaches senior status, don't stop purposeful playtime with him. Make it your quest to provide him with age-appropriate environmental enrichments that make his life more fulfilling. And there is a medical benefit to this. The stress of living a boring, monotonous life can contribute to a senior cat becoming stressed and developing urinary tract infections or bladder infections.

Simply, tone down your cat's favourite activities. Engage your elderly cat in stalking a feather wand toy across the floor instead of waving it up in the air for him to try to leap for. Making snake-like manoeuvres on the floor with this wand toy will prevent jolts to his aged joints.

Let your vet know how often your cat is jumping and precisely how high. You may think that after 12 years, you finally taught your cat not to jump on the kitchen worktop. Instead, the sad reality is that your cat has developed osteoarthritis and can no longer reach the counter from the floor.

Just like in people, senior cats are at risk for age-related conditions, including diabetes and arthritis.

Feline Dementia

Your elderly cat may not seem to be as 'with it' mentally and begin to display some bizarre behaviours, such as seeming to be trapped in a corner. Senior cats need to be observed with regular care and attention.

As our beloved pets transition from seniors to geriatrics, they are also susceptible to age-related conditions, including arthritis, diabetes, heart disease and cognitive dysfunction, similar to Alzheimer's disease in people. Cognitive dysfunction (also known as dementia or senility) is a neurological disorder of older cats characterised by a decline in cognitive ability due to brain ageing.

I remember the first time I spotted my 19-year-old cat, Little Guy, looking confused in a corner of my living room. He appeared to be lost. He also began vocalising more with a mournful miaow that seemed to say, 'Where am I?' At the time, I wasn't sure what was happening to him, but now I do. Little Guy had developed feline dementia, also known as feline cognitive dysfunction. He lived to be 20 and, during his final year, I trained all guests to gently guide this brown-striped tabby out of corners and to sweetly answer, 'Little Guy, over here' whenever he began making those sorrowful howls. In people years, he lived to be 96 years old.

Some cats and dogs start to exhibit certain telltale signs of cognitive dysfunction around age 12. Veterinary and behavioural experts use the acronym DISH to refer to the symptoms and signs commonly associated with canine or feline senility.

'D' IS FOR DISORIENTED.

Pets who are disoriented often walk aimlessly, stare at walls or get stuck in corners.

'I' IS FOR INTERACTIONS.

Pets with impaired mental function often become less likely to greet people when they come home or seek out a lap.

If your geriatric cat begins urinating or defecating outside the litter box, it may be a sign of senility.

When it is time to say farewell to your terminally ill cat, make sure all members of the household are present for the euthanasia process, even other family pets.

'S' IS FOR SLEEP.

Cats who once slept soundly through the night may prowl or pace restlessly at night and may vocalise as they roam.

'H' IS FOR HOUSETRAINING.

Some cats suddenly forget to use the litter box and piddle on the floor.

If your cat is exhibiting any of these signs, please have your vet perform a thorough examination that will include blood and urine tests. Your golden oldie may have a physical condition that could be treated with medicine or at least slowed down.

Sadly, there is no cure for cognitive dysfunction in our pets – yet. We can't put the brakes on the number of birthdays our pets accumulate, but we can take purposeful steps to keep them feeling years younger. Veterinary researchers are learning ways to manage senility with memory-improving medications and specially formulated senior diets.

Know When to Say Goodbye

Knowing when to say goodbye to your terminally ill cat is never easy. We love our pets and we do struggle with end-of-life issues. Veterinary associations have created senior care guidelines for dogs and cats. These guidelines identify 5 'freedoms' to help determine if euthanasia is warranted:

- Freedom from hunger and thirst
- Freedom from physical and thermal discomfort
- Freedom from pain, injury and disease
- Freedom from fear and distress
- Freedom to express normal behaviour

Think of four or five things that your cat really likes to do and that give him his personality. Then realise that when those things start to go away, then your cat is also going away mentally and physically. You reach a point where the cat you know is not there anymore. Euthanasia is a gift of love, the last gift you can give your beloved pet.

Adopting a Senior Cat

You can make the golden years of a cat's life truly golden ones by adopting a senior cat at your local animal shelter. Each day, he can enrich your life.

Thinking about adopting a cat or two? Give special consideration to felines who have surpassed their seventh birthdays and beyond. By doing so, you save your sanity by skipping the crazy kittenhood time. Let me happily share five reasons to adopt a senior cat:

PREDICTABLE PERSONALITIES.

If you adopt a senior cat who is a sweet cat, you will have a sweet cat when you take him home. The personality has been developed, so there are no surprises. What you see is what you get.

THEY GENERALLY DO NOT DEVIATE IN SIZE OR APPETITE.

Whether you adopted a petite or a gigantic-sized senior cat, you will know exactly how much food and litter you need to buy.

CHAMPIONS OF POWER NAPS.

Kittens have so much energy and can disrupt your sleep at night. On the other hand, senior cats are far calmer and enjoy sleeping a lot. You stand a better chance of enjoying a full night's sleep.

MORE MELLOW THAN MISCHIEVOUS.

Kittens and young cats can be so fearless, so you have to worry more about them ingesting string or other foreign bodies or suffering from a trauma. That's not so much the case with wiser senior cats.

YOU WILL BE SAVING A LIFE AND MAKING WAY FOR ANOTHER TO WIN A HOME.

When you adopt a senior cat from a shelter, you earn major karma points in my view. You are also making it possible for the shelter to showcase other strays to help them find homes.

If you don't have the time – or patience – to raise a young kitten, consider adopting a mellow senior cat.

HOW OLD IS YOUR CAT?

Forget the notion that one cat year equals 7 human years. It is a myth without merit. Leading vets and animal behaviourists contend that a 1-year-old cat is comparative in age to a 15-year-old person. After the first 2 years, each passing year for your cat is the equivalent of 4 human years.

AGE OF CAT	HUMAN AGE EQUIVALENT
1	15
2	24
3	28
4	32
5	36
6	40
7	44
8	48
9	52
10	56
11	60
12	64
13	68
14	72
15	76
16	80
17	84
18	88
19	92
20	96

WORLD'S OLDEST CAT

The current record holder for being the Methuselah of cats was a British tabby named Puss who died in 1939 at the astounding age of 36.

Feline Trivia

To know your cat better, it is vital that you are able to separate feline fact from fiction. Here are some surprising catty truths.

CATS PUT THE 'C' IN COLOUR.

Cats come in more than 75 different colours and patterns – beyond white, black and brown, some sport shades of red, orange, silver, lilac and other hues.

CATS ARE FURRY RIP VAN WINKLES.

Indoor cats sleep nearly two-thirds of every day – up to about 18 hours a day. Only opossums and bats snooze more – about 20 hours a day.

SOME CATS ACTUALLY LIKE TO GET WET.

Turkish Vans hail from Lake Van and earned the nickname 'the swimming cat'. Bengals also are drawn to water and have surprised some of their owners by joining them in the shower.

OLYDACTYL IS NOT A DISEASE.

Most cats are born with five toes on each front paw and four toes on each back paw. However, a genetic mutation occurs in some cats, causing them to sport extra toes on each paw – a benign condition called polydactyl. These mega-toed cats were highly sought after by sea-faring ships because the extra toes gave them better grips on the ship's decks, making them agile mousers.

CATS ENGAGE THEIR PURRING MECHANISM FOR THREE REASONS.

It is well recognised that cats purr when they feel contented, making a rumbling sound that resembles an idling diesel engine. Because newborn kittens are born blind, a mother cat will purr so that the vibrations act as a homing signal to orient the kittens towards her at feeding time. Finally, some cats purr when they are sick or even in the process of dying as a self-calming technique.

LEARN THE LINGO

A pack of kittens is called a kindle (the term was associated with felines long before e-books were invented) but a group of adult cats is referred to as a clowder. A female cat is called a queen or a Molly.

You can try but never completely succeed at mastering the art of the purr because cats are also the only species capable of purring while inhaling and exhaling.

A CAT'S TONGUE CONTAINS ROWS OF BARBS CALLED FILIFORM PAPILLAE.

Barbs are the reason behind the sandpaper-like texture of your cat's tongue. These barbs are positioned towards the throat and designed to help a cat hold a prey, like a mouse, in her mouth while eating.

CATS OUTTALK DOGS 10 TO 1.

Cats can make more than 100 distinctive vocalisations (compared to about 10 sounds for dogs), but these sounds are mostly directed at people because they rarely miaow at other cats. And cats outhear dogs. Cats can hear up to 100,000 Hz, compared to dogs at between 35,000 and 40,000 Hz. People can hear up to 20,000 Hz.

CATS ARE SPEEDY AND SPRINGY.

A house cat can reach speeds of 30 mph and jump up to seven times their height from a sitting position. The fastest domesticated cat breed on record is the Egyptian Mau, clocked at 36 mph.

IN DIM LIGHT, THE EYES OF CATS GIVE OFF A GHOULISH GLOW.

Causing this glow is a group of light-sensitive cells located behind the retinas known as the *tapetum lucidum* – a Latin term meaning 'bright carpet' – that allows cats to take in extra light in dimly lit situations. These special cells enable cats to quickly adapt to low-light conditions, a necessity for these nocturnal hunters.

HISTORICAL CATS

Garfield, the lasagna-loving cartoon cat created by Jim Davis, is certainly well known. So are the Internet sensations Grumpy Cat and Maru. But here are a few felines whose accomplishments may surprise you:

FELICETTE

This cat earned the nickname Astrocat by becoming the first feline launched into outer space in 1963 by the French. She had electrodes implanted into her brain so that her neural impulses could be recorded. After a 15-minute trip in space, Felicette parachuted safely back to Earth.

SNOWBALL

This white cat had extra toes and belonged to a ship's captain who gave her as a gift to noted author Ernest Hemingway when he and his wife, Pauline, moved into their Key West, Florida, home. Snowball is the matriarch of the generations of polydactyl cats enjoying a life of leisure at the Hemingway Home, which is now a major tourist attraction.

PUSS

This British cat landed in the record books as the oldest cat. She died in 1939 at the grand old age of 36.

STUBBS

This cat was a write-in candidate and was elected mayor of Talkeetna, Alaska, in 1997.

UNSINKABLE SAM

This tabby survived three shipwrecks while aboard military ships during World War II.

Further Reading

BOOKS BY ARDEN MOORE:

❧ *The Cat Behaviour Answer Book*
   Storey Publishing, 2007

❧ *Happy Cat, Happy You*
   Storey Publishing, 2008

❧ *The Kitten Owner's Manual*
   Storey Publishing, 2001

BOOKS RECOMMENDED BY ARDEN MOORE:

❧ *The Healing Power of Pets*
   by Dr. Marty Becker with Danelle Morton
   Hyperion Books, 2003

❧ *Outsmarting Cats* by Wendy Christensen
   Globe Pequot Press, 2013

❧ *Catification: Designing a Happy and
   Stylish Home for Your Cat (and You)*
   by Jackson Galaxy and Kate Benjamin
   Jeremy P Tarcher, 2014

❧ *What's the Matter with Henry? The True
   Tale of a Three-Legged Cat* by Cathy
   Conheim and BJ Gallagher
   Breakthrough Press, 2013

❧ *Naughty No More* by Marilyn Krieger
   BowTie Press, 2011

❧ *Does This Collar Make My Butt Look Big?
   A Diet Book for Cats*
   by Dena Harris
   Ten Speed Press, 2013

ABOUT ARDEN MOORE:

Arden Moore – The Pawsitive Coach™ –
happily wears many 'collars' in the pet world:
radio show host, author, professional
speaker, editor, media consultant, dog/cat
behaviour consultant and master pet first-aid
instructor.

Arden is the founder of Four Legged Life,
an online pet community, and creator of
National Dog Party Day, an annual event that
raises money for pet charities and brings out
the playful party animal in people and their
dogs. As an in-demand pet safety, behaviour
and lifestyle expert, Arden is on a mission:
to bring out the best in pets and their people.
She shares her home with two dogs, two
cats and an overworked vacuum cleaner.
Learn more at www.fourleggedlife.com.

Index

Picture Credits